Contents

Chapter 1: Welcome & Planning Ahead for 2025 - 3
Chapter 2: Using the Calendar - 5
Chapter 3: Reading the Calendar Layout - 7
Chapter 4: Text Ephemeris, Planetary Speed, Void of Course - 9
Chapter 5: About the Signs - 11
Chapter 6: About the Planets - 13
Chapter 7: About the Aspects - 15
Chapter 8: About the Calendar's Astrology - 17
Chapter 9: BioDynamic Gardening & Wine Tasting - 18
Chapter 10: Reclaiming Astrology from the Patriarchy - 19
Chapter 11: A Peek at 2026 - 21

The Monthly Forecasts & Calendars

January - 22	**July - 46**
February - 26	**August - 50**
March - 30	**September -**
April - 34	**October - 58**
May - 38	**November - 62**
June - 42	**December - 66**

Ephemeris Grids - 70
Quick Reference Pages
Retrogrades & Eclipses - 82
Timing with the Planets - 83
Signs & Planetary Rulers - 84
The Catalog & Ordering the 2026 Planetary Calendar - 85-86

The 2025 Planetary Astrology Calendar
Pocket Edition with Forecasts Calculated for Pacific Time
By Ralph & Lahni DeAmicis

Planetary Calendar, an Imprint of
Cuore Libre Publishing
Napa, California
www.PlanetaryCalendar.com

Copyright 2025 Ralph & Lahni DeAmicis
ISBN 979-8-3303-4069-9
No part of this calendar may be reproduced in
any form without permission from the publisher.

Spiral Galaxy Cover Photo Credits: NASA & JPL

The Planetary Calendar is calculated in Solar Fire using Pacific 'Clock Time', so it adapts to Daylight Savings Time. Adjustments for the other North American time zones are found at the bottom of the 'Month at a Glance' pages. The charts are calculated for Sacramento, the capitol of California. We use this region not only because it is the center of our universe, but because the North Bay is one the longest continuously occupied regions in North America, so it clearly has good Feng Shui!

Disclaimer: Even though we make every effort to get the correct information into the correct places, there are thousands of data points, so errors occur. Also, we make every effort to provide trustworthy forecasts, based on generally accepted Astrological principles, but forecasting is, by its nature, subject to undetected influences that may skew the results. Therefore, we accept no responsibility for any losses or inconveniences you may suffer from using this information, although we truly hope you find it helpful.

Welcome to the Planetary Astrology Calendar

For New Users: Please Read the Instructions. This unique and simple system will help you effectively time meetings, events and travel to get the best results.

For returning users: Despite saying that we were not making any changes, sorry, we've made improvements. As before, when a Planet makes an Aspect to the Moon, they are shown above or below the Date, but now they are preceded by the Aspect.

The monthly forecasts are longer and include the date plus the time span of the Retrogrades. When there is a problematic Void of Course Moon, now a light Gray Box appears on the Date. Due to an update in our design software, we were forced to use a less than ideal astrology font so as not to delay the 2025 edition. We will take the time for a complete rebuild of the calendar in new software so we can use a better font and update the old illustrations for 2026. PLEASE NOTE: Our contact information has also changed. (See inside back cover)

Visit PlanetaryCalendar.com/instructions for details.

All versions include the monthly calendar pages, a monthly text ephemeris, symbol guide, annotated forecasts, instructions, a scientific ephemeris and Quick Reference Pages. The Day Planner and Digital Version also include Lunation Charts and the Day Planner includes 'Week-At-A-Glance' pages for appointments or notes.

Strategizing the Year Ahead: Eclipses: Avoid planning stressful events like weddings, travel and medical procedures between Eclipses. This year the first pair runs from March 13th to March 29th, and the second pair runs from September 7th to September 22nd. If these align with your major Planets, take special care during those times.

Mercury Retrogrades: During those nine weeks avoid purchases of phones, transportation and electronics. They run from March 14th to April 7th, from July 17th to August 11th, and from November 9th to November 29th. Refer to the Retrograde and Eclipse tables on the Quick Reference Pages.

A Look at the Year Ahead: The year starts off slowly with Mars, Jupiter and Uranus Retrograde, so getting projects moving may take extra work. The New Moon on **January** 29th begins **the Year of the Wood Snake**. This is a good time to focus on personal issues more than social. Uranus turns Direct at the end of January and Jupiter at the beginning of **February**, so events will pick up later in the month. **March** is complicated by two Eclipses, Mercury and Venus turning Retrograde and Neptune entering Aries where it will be until 2029. Neptune was last in Aries between 1862 and 1875. During that time was the American Civil War, the end of slavery, the first transcontinental railroad, the purchase of Alaska from the Russian Empire, and the legal case that determined that States could not leave the Union.
April will be easier as Mercury and Venus turn Direct and Mars enters Leo. In **May**, Pluto turns Retrograde, but the big event is Saturn entering Aries, so expect a shift in expectations. In **June** only Pluto is Retrograde so events will progress quickly and smoothly. The big event is Jupiter entering its Exalted, Colleague Sign of Cancer. As Jupiter Squares Saturn, expect big economic news. In **July**, the big event is Uranus entering Gemini. The last time it was there was during WWII, and it always seems to boost the fight for human rights into high gear. **August** is a milder month helped by a fast-moving Jupiter.

An eventful **September** starts with Saturn backing into Pisces, Uranus turning Retrograde, followed by two Eclipses and the Fall Equinox. In **October** Neptune backs into Pisces while Pluto turns Direct. Mercury and Mars are moving quickly so take advantage of that physicality to get practical tasks done. **November** is packed with events including Jupiter turning Retrograde, Saturn turning Direct, and Uranus backing into Taurus. In **December** Neptune turns Direct while the personal Planets make good progress, so the calendar year ends smoothly.

Wishing You Good Stars in this Interesting Year Ahead.

Ralph & Lahni DeAmicis

Two: Using the Calendar

Start by looking at the whole Day Block and divide it into four quadrants. When there are more Planetary Glyphs above the Date Number (Lunar Aspects) it indicates an easier social day. More Glyphs below make for a challenging day. More Glyphs above the Dotted Line (Planetary Aspects) indicate helpful connections in the outer world. Aspects below indicate challenges.

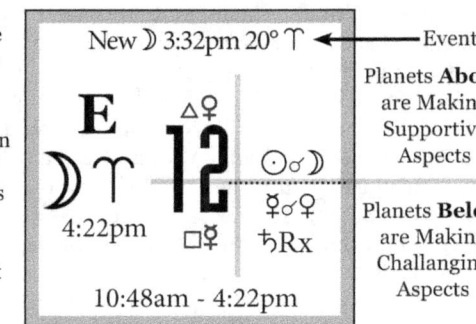

On the **Left** are the Moon's Sign and the Lunar Aspects

On the **Right** are Aspects to the Sun and the Planets

A Frame denotes a New Moon, Full Moon & the Sun's Ingress into the Next Sign

Events

Planets **Above** are Making Supportive Aspects

Planets **Below** are Making Challanging Aspects

A Void of Course Moon ends when it enters the Next Sign

These four quadrants reflect the design of the human body. The upper body optimistically focuses on the future while the lower deals with the results. Your head thinks, 'Let's go for a walk', but it's your feet that are sore later! The left side of the body is the Lunar, emotional side, while the right is the Solar, more social side. The left is where you hold a baby's head, so they hear your heartbeat, but it's your right hand that you extend in greeting.

The 'upper' supportive Aspects are the Conjunction (0 degrees), Sextile (60 degrees) and Trine (120 degrees). The 'lower' or challenging Aspects are the Square (90 degrees) and the Opposition (180 degrees). When a day has mostly supportive Aspects, we mark it with a **White Circle**. When the challenging Aspects dominate, we put a **Black Box** around the Date. A **Light Gray Box** denotes a long, problematic Void of Course Moon. A **Gray Frame** found on a Day Block denotes the New Moon, Full Moon and the Sun's entrance (Ingress) into the next Sign. You can read about the Aspects to better understand their diverse influences in Section Seven.

Find your Sun Sign, Ruling Planet, and its Glyph on the quick reference pages at the back to personalize your experience of the Calendar. When your Glyph appears above the Date, the day will feel easier as the Moon supports your talents. When it is below, you have to work harder to make things come out right. **Note: Cancer and Leo Sun Positions.** The Sun and Moon do not appear above and below the Date, so Cancerians instead use Venus, the Ruler of feminine Taurus, the Sign of the Moon's Exaltation. The Leos use Mars, the Ruler of masculine Aries, the Sign of the Sun's Exaltation. The way we describe the Exalted position is as the 'Best Friend' or "Colleague".

When your Planetary Ruler appears above or below the Dotted Line, that Planet is making a significant connection with another Planet, indicating important things are happening in your life. While Aspects above the Line are supportive and below are challenging, the nature of the Planets and the Aspect that connects them will shape how it affects you. Planetary Aspects are felt for extended periods and the slower the Planet, the longer the duration of those effects. For example, Mercury to Venus Aspects may last a few days, while Saturn to Neptune Aspects can last weeks or longer. Read the pages about the Planets and the Aspects for a greater understanding of those differences.

Three: Reading the Calendar Layout

The Upper Page

On either side of the Month and Year you will see the Signs that begin and end each month. Below that is the Forecast with the Capital Footnote (A) referencing the Dates on the Grid. The Forecast provides insights into the Planetary Transits, Direction changes (Retrograde or Direct) and Aspects. At the bottom of the page is the Glyph to English Key with Keywords to make understanding the calendar easier. See the expanded descriptions of the Signs, Planets and Aspects in the related chapters.

The Lower Page

The Compact Text Ephemeris shows the Planetary Positions by Sign and Degree on the first day of the month, in plain language. It also shows any Planetary Sign changes and direction changes (Retrograde or Direct). There is a classic Table Ephemeris for the year after December, but the Compact Ephemeris is a quick reference for Planetary positions. At the bottom margin are calculations for four continental USA Time Zones. The Calendar is calculated for Pacific 'Clock' Time. There is no need to adjust your calculation for Daylight Savings Time unless your State does not use it.

The only Lunar Aspects shown on the line are to the Sun. The Planetary Direction changes are also shown on the Dotted Line, 'D' for Direct is above the line and 'Rx' for Retrograde is below. The White Circle denotes a day with mostly supportive Aspects, when new projects encounter minimum resistance. The Black Box around the Date denotes a day with challenging Aspects when new projects may require extra work. A Gray Frame denotes the Lunations.

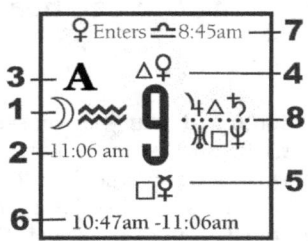

What the Day Blocks Signify

Use the Date in the center as your reference

1) To the left is the symbol for the Moon and its current Sign.
2) Below that is the time when the Moon enters that Sign.
3) Above that is a letter that footnotes to the forecast. e.g '**A**'.
4) Above are the supportive Aspects (Conjunction, Sextile, Trine).
5) Below are the challenging Aspects (Square, Opposition).
The Lunar Aspects Above & Below the Date run
 from left to right, as they occur from early to late.
6) At the lower edge of the Box are the times of the Moon's Void
of Course (VOC) see pg. 31, which can span multiple days.
7) At the top edge of each box are the Planetary Ingresses,
Lunations, Eclipses, Meteors and Holidays.
8) To the right of the Date on the Dotted Line are the Planetary
Aspects. Supportive Aspects are above and Challenging Aspects are
below. Their time sequence runs from the Dotted Line up or Dotted
Line down, with the earliest Aspects touching the Line.

Four: Text Ephemeris, Planetary Speed & VOC

The Text Ephemeris is easy to read because everything is in English and each planets motions are described. There is a full Ephemeris after December for long range planning. The Text Ephemeris shows the month's Planetary Movements, Sign and Direction changes, with degrees. The Solar and Lunar changes are shown in the Day Blocks. The Sun entering a new Sign and the New Moon and Full Moon are highlighted with a Gray Frame.

> Mercury☿ 10° Capricorn♑ enters Aquarius♒ on the 13th at 9:51am. Venus♀Rx 20° Capricorn♑. Mars♂ 21° Scorpio♏, enters Sagittarius♐ on the 13th at 1:52am. Jupiter♃ 25° Aquarius♒ enters Pisces♓ on the 28th at 8:09pm. Saturn♄ 8° Aquarius♒. Uranus♅Rx 11° Taurus♉. Neptune♆Rx 20° Pisces♓. Pluto♇ 25° Capricorn♑.

Start projects between the New and Full Moon because energy is rising. The Sun Trine Moon after the Full Moon (Waning Gibbous) is when the energy is flowing most smoothly so that's a good time to overcome resistance. As Planets prepare to change Direction they slow from our perspective and issues related to them in our world will be harder to move forward.

When the Planets are moving fast, you have the wind at your back. Everything related to them happens more quickly and easily. That is why it is important to understand what each Planet signifies. In our Forecasts, we also take into account the speed of the Planets as indicators.

Some Planets change Sign and Direction more often. Here is a quick guide to each Planet's orbit.

Mercury: 88 days; **Venus**: 224.7 days; **Earth**: 365.256 days; **Mars**: 687 days; **Jupiter**: 11.86 years; **Saturn**: 29.5 years; **Uranus**: 84 years; **Neptune**: 164.8 years; **Pluto**: 248 years

While the inner Planets affect our daily lives, outer Planets affect our social standing. For example, Jupiter Returns to your birth position at ages 12, 24, 36, etc., often lucky years. Saturn takes 29.5 years to 'Return', once the average lifespan, thus Saturn's connection to maturity. The current lifespan is 78 years, closer to the orbit of Uranus, although with its 84-year orbit, many people never experience their Uranus Return. Our experience of Uranus, Neptune and Pluto, with their long orbits, is less personal and more gradual, often intangible. We imagine them like our utilities; they exist in the background and we don't notice them until the power, water or internet go out.

About the Void of Course (VOC) Moon

The period after the Moon's last Aspect to any Planet, until it enters the next Sign, is the *Void of Course*. Ugly Void of Course periods are marked with a Gray Box around the date so you don't miss them. Some people have more of a problem than others with that event. To understand the VOC, imagine the Moon as someone running between meetings who finds themselves at loose ends until the next appointment. While this time may be potentially unproductive, it can also be a very creative time because it lacks an agenda. Also, some VOC periods are better than others. When the Moon is in Signs Ruled by Jupiter (**Sagittarius & Pisces**) or its own Rulership & Exaltation, **(Cancer & Taurus)** she is self-directed and resourceful so that time is less challenging.

Five: About the Signs

To use the Calendar effectively you will need to know your Sun Sign and its Ruling Planet. It's important to understand what the Twelve Signs represent beyond the annual sequence of nature's seasons.

Planets are defined in four ways and each is a unique combination of those definitions: Polarity, Element, Quality and Planetary Ruler. The two Polarities are Masculine and Feminine. We can also call them Dynamic and Responsive.

Then there are the Four Elements: Fire, Earth, Air and Water. These represent the four States of Matter in physics: Plasma, Solid, Gaseous and Liquid. Masculine Fire energizes, Feminine Earth stabilizes, Masculine Air interacts and Feminine Water dissolves.

The Three Qualities represent the stages within the annual cycle of the seasons: Cardinal initiates, Fixed systemizes and Mutable humanizes.

The Planets are related to the Signs in complex ways described by the Table of Planetary Dignities. Each Planet has six Signs that it relates to most directly, but in the Calendar we want you to use what is called the Planet's 'Ruling' Signs, the most socially active Dynamic and Responsive positions.

We use the classic, traditional Rulers, so there are no Rulerships assigned to Uranus, Neptune or Pluto. If you learned Astrology in the fifties, sixties and seventies, this may seem bizarre but the Astrologers who assigned the 'modern' Rulers had limited understanding of the underlying Geometry at work. They also had almost no data on the newly discovered Planets to base those decisions.

That means both **Aries** and **Scorpio** will look for **Mars** above or below the Date and Dotted Line in the Day Blocks as an indicator about the day. **Sagittarius** and **Pisces** will look for **Jupiter**. **Capricorn** and **Aquarius** will look for **Saturn**.

The Twelve Signs
Planetary Ruler, Quality, Element, Action, Opposite Sign

♈ **Aries**: ♂ Mars, Cardinal, Fire, Initiates, ♎
The symbol is the Ram. They are energetic.

♉ **Taurus**: ♀ Venus, Fixed, Earth, Stabilizes, ♏
The symbol is the Bull. They are patient.

♊ **Gemini**: ☿ Mercury, Mutable, Air, Interacts, ♐
The symbol is the Twins are in arm. They are engaging.

♋ **Cancer**: ♂ Moon, Cardinal, Water, Nurtures, ♑
The symbol is the Crabs. They are protective.

♌ **Leo**: ☉ Sun, Fixed, Fire, Creates, ♒
The symbol is the Lion. They are dramatic.

♍ **Virgo**: ☿ Mercury, Mutable, Earth, Perfect, ♓
The symbol is the Virgin. They are diligent.

♎ **Libra:** ♀ Venus, Cardinal, Air, Balances, ♈
The symbol is the Scales. They are considerate.

♏ **Scorpio**: ♂ Mars, Fixed, Water, Manages, ♉
The symbol is the Scorpion. They are daring.

♐ **Sagittarius**: ♃ Jupiter, Mutable, Fire, Optimizes, ♊
The symbol is the Centaur's bow & arrow. They are confident.

♑ **Capricorn**: ♄ Saturn, Cardinal, Earth, Codifies, ♋
The symbol is the Sea Goat. They are dependable.

♒ **Aquarius**: ♄ Saturn, Fixed, Air, Innovates, ♌
The symbol is the Water Bearer. They are revolutionary.

♓ **Pisces**: ♃ Jupiter, Mutable, Water, Unites, ♍
The symbol is the Fishes. They are philosophical.

Six: About the Planets

The Calendar shows the every changing dynamics between the Planets and how they influence us through these Aspects. Our descriptions of the Planets are about the nature of the energy that they bring to those meetings. To understand the Planets you need to see them in their various guises and that is what our Table of Dignities reveals. In the same way that we act differently at work or home, with friends or family, the Planets each have six roles they play on the Astrological stage. They have three Social roles: the two Rulers and the Exaltation, and three Personal roles: the two Detriments and the Fall.

To learn more, read the Calendar's Companion Book for a non-misogynistic explanation of this vital interpretation tool. To that end, we have replaced Masculine and Feminine with Dynamic and Resposive. When Planets are in Aspect, the 'current' is flowing. If you jump into projects when the Aspects are Supportive, you can ride the tides. If you start when they are Challenging, you'll be bucking the flow.

How Planets Act When they Make a Connection

When the **Sun** makes an Aspect, it brings energy to that Planet. When Supportive, it promotes stability. When Challenged, it bullies. The Sun's Dynamic Ruling Sign is Leo; Cancer is its Receptive Ruler and Aries is its Exaltation. In those Signs, the Sun lives for the outer, social world. In the opposite Signs, Aquarius, Capricorn and Libra, the Sun is concerned for the personal life.

When the **Moon** makes an Aspect, it lends emotional oomph to the relationship. Supportive; it's a helping hand. Challenged; it's a slap. The Social Trilogy is Cancer, Sagittarius and Taurus. The Personal Trilogy is Capricorn, Gemini and Scorpio.

When **Mercury** connects it promotes engagement. Supportive; it provides good information. Challenged; it teases and tests.
When **Venus** connects, beauty and indulgence arrive. Supportive; it's graceful and artistic. Challenged; it is indulgent.
When **Mars** connects passions heat up. Supportive; it is protective, engaging. Challenged; defensive, destructive.
When **Jupiter** connects horizons, possibilities & imagination expand. Supportive; it rescues. Challenged; it runs roughshod.
When **Saturn** connects it provides maturity, discipline, structure. Supportive; a protective wall. Challenged; a limiting fence.
When **Uranus** connects it electrifies, networks & communicates. Supportive; it is a community. Challenged; it is a gang.
When **Neptune** connects it expands us beyond the visible. Supportive; new levels of perception. Challenged; confusion.
When **Pluto** connects it amplifies, intensifies. Supportive; strong gets stronger. Challenged; magnifies the weaknesses.

Seven: About the Aspects

Aspects are the angles made between the Sun, Moon, Planets, Ascendant and Midheaven. As an Astrological tool, it's like a family tree crossed with a wiring diagram. While individual Planets show a person's talents, the Aspects show the Planets either working in concert (Conjunct 0°), being mutually supportive (Sextile 60° & Trine 120°), or being demanding (Square 90° & Opposition 180°). A less used Aspect is the Parallel, that shows when Planets have a similar status.

Conjunction - 0 to 7 Degrees - The Planets are close together, deciding and working in concert.

Sextile - 60 Degrees - Polarity, the Sextile creates an easy, supportive relationship, like cousins working and playing together.

Square - 90 Degrees - Imagine cars meeting at an intersection. The drivers must use the rules and their wits to get where they're going and avoid crashing.

Trine - 120 Degrees - This harmonious, strongly supportive connection is like siblings who provide the muscle and resources each other needs without question.

Opposition - 180 Degrees - Imagine two people sitting opposite each other negotiating. While each is committed to their position, they need something from each other.

Parallel - 0 degrees of Latitude - This notes Planets equally North or South of the Ecliptic, holding equal status, or rank. By itself it's not significant, but it eases the way for any other Aspect. The related Aspect, the Contra Parallel, which is marked by the parallel lines with an angled line crossing them, represents Planets at opposite distances above and below the Ecliptic. This describes a mentor relationship in which the lower Planet is the beneficiary of the upper. We don't list the Contra Parallel, although we consider it in our forecasts.

When evaluating Aspects, consider what each Planet does for the other:

The Sun energizes,   the Moon comforts,
Mercury engages,   Venus charms,
Mars confronts,   Jupiter expands,
Saturn compresses,   Uranus disrupts,
Neptune envisions   and Pluto empowers.

The Aspects determine how they contribute. The Conjunction unifies. The Sextile and Trine help without causing trouble. The Square and Opposition build and noisily bang into each other, because that's the nature of work.

The Aspects involving the Sun, Moon, Mercury, Venus, Mars and the Ascendant are felt personally. Those involving Jupiter, Saturn and the Midheaven are experienced socially. Aspects involving Uranus, Neptune and Pluto are felt gradually, because they change Signs so slowly, maintaining Aspects for long periods.

Outer planet Aspects are like sitting on a boat deck with friends and a big bottle of wine, enjoying the afternoon turning into evening. As the tide rolls in and the boat gradually rises, no one notices. It's only later, as they step down to the dock, that they'll recognize the change. Outer Planet Aspects are a different experience from the inner Planetary Aspects that say, *'Bam! Wake Up, Mars is Here!'*

Eight: About the Calendar's Astrology

The calendar's simplified astrology uses three components: the Planets, who are the actors, the Signs of the Tropical Zodiac, that describe the actions, and the geometric Aspects that are the relationships between the Planets. The fourth major part of an Astrological Chart is the House System, that brings the Planets down to Earth. While we use Whole Sign Houses when creating the written Forecasts, they are not considerations in the data we put in the Day Blocks.

An Astrological Chart is a cosmic weather report. In the same way that a TV meteorologist tells you the current weather based on a specific time and place we calculate Astrology Charts for the exact minute. Just like weather forecasts, Astrology forecasts are based on the laws of physics and observation.

Astrologers have been observing the influence of the heavenly Planets on the Earth below for thousands of generations. The Astronomical ephemeris shows us where the Planets will be in the future, and we can look for when those patterns appeared in the past. When we know what happened historically at that time, we get clues about possible events in the future.

Astrology Calendars are different than Charts, because they are about the ongoing movement of the Planets and the relationships they form and dissolve during the evolving year. In the forecasts, we make a big deal when a slow-moving Planet like Jupiter, Saturn or Pluto changes Sign, because a long-running agenda in larger economic or social movements is going to change.

Nine: BioDynamic Gardening

Biodynamic organic farming was developed in the 1920's in response to the wide-scale use of chemicals in farming following WWI. It uses an Astrological Gardening Calendar to time tasks in the field.

Water Moon Days are good for leaf plants like lettuce, spinach, celery and cabbage. Cancer, Scorpio, Pisces.

Fire Moon Days are good for fruits, nuts, seeds and gourds like cherries, pumpkins, oranges. Aries, Leo, Sagittarius.

Earth Moon Days are good for root vegetables and storing crops. Taurus, Virgo, Capricorn.

Air Moon Days are good for flowering plants and medicinal herbs like mints and basil. Gemini, Libra, Aquarius.

The New Moon is for resting, celebration and meditation.

The Full Moon is for celebration and harvesting all crops, especially medicinal plants.

Wine Tasting

The flavors of wine come from the fruit and are perceived through the nose and palate. Both the Fire (Fruit) Moon (Aries, Leo, Sagittarius) and the Air (Flower) Moon (Gemini, Libra, Aquarius) tend to bring out the subtle, more nuanced notes in the wines. The Earth Moon (Taurus, Virgo, Capricorn) favor serious, aged wines with deep earthy qualities, while the Water Moon (Cancer, Scorpio, Pisces) can add a lighter, smoother quality, loosening up an otherwise stiff varietal wine. See our book, 'Wine Tasting with the Stars' for more.

Ten: Reclaiming Astrology from the Patriarchy

This is a Speech and New Book by Drs. Ralph & Lahni DeAmicis

The Zodiac is humanity's oldest teaching tool, an unchanging blackboard that the elders once used to teach the young how to find food by adjusting to natures cycles. The original symbols, chosen by the Egyptians, reflected the balance of nature, and this produced a society where men and women had equal rights.

Where did this go wrong? It happened because Astrology, like celestial navigation, is based on the geometry of the solar system as seen from Earth. Twenty-five hundred years ago, the highly patriarchal Greeks broke that geometry to favor men, and it took western society off course.

The Greeks then taught their astrology to the Romans, who broke the geometry even more and then rebranded the symbols of the Zodiac. The early Roman priests changed the Zodiac into a propaganda tool that promoted the Empire and their new male dominated Catholic church. They changed all but one of the feminine Signs, while debating whether women had souls. At the time, the largest and wealthiest temple in the Roman Forum was dedicated to Venus, and the priests wanted her money.

For the next fifteen hundred years the practice of Astrology was thoroughly screwed up. And then, in the early twentieth century a group of writers and psychics made it even worse. They were so steeped in that patriarchy, and confused by the broken geometry, that they smashed the system into pieces. As a result, astrology further relegated women to disempowered societal roles, where they would get little credit for their efforts.

For us to use this broken, patriarchal system today when eighty percent of astrologers, and their clients, are women is nonsensical. By restoring the geometry and invoking the true, balanced symbols, we can improve people's self-image and society's balance. Astrology is an ancient system that evolves with its culture.

So, there is no reason we cannot hit the reset, toss out these illogical, unbalanced changes, and restore the Goddess to her proper ascendancy. We know who broke the system, how they broke it and why they did that. Restoring it to its original elegant and graceful design is easier than you might think. Expect the book in 2024. Arrange a speech at PlanetaryCalendar.com.

The Twelve True Signs

Spring: The Lamb, The Cow, The Twin Baby Goats

Summer: The Crab, The Lion, The Great Goddess

Fall: The Scales, The Eagle, The Archer

Winter: The Sea Lion, The Irrigator, The Great Lady of the Zodiac, Her Son & Two Porpoises,

Eleven: Here's a Peek at 2026!

The New Moon on February 17th begins the Year of the Fire Horse, always a lively time and this is looking like an especially exciting year. The attention of the world shifts away from the USA and towards Europe. France, England, Ireland, Spain and Portugal may be the center of a disruptive global youth movement focused on human rights and climate change. Italy is looking at a financially good year although, expect to see a very active women's rights movement there.

The wars in Ukraine and Gaza will be especially harsh, but the global community will be actively enforcing rules and limits on the conflicts. There will be a shared sense that the ego centered patriarchy that is directing these onslaughts is poisoning the spiritual health of the planet and damaging global economies. Japan and Australia will both see expansions that benefit their local economies.

The USA East Coast will see an enthusiastic emergence of a new community of younger political leaders willing to make broad changes. Expect women's rights to be a clarion call. The West will be generally more peaceful with the Southwest having good economic progress by returning to previous International partnerships, especially with Japan, Australia and the Pacific Rim. The Bay Area will be a site of activism related to family and children's issues. The center of the country will see both climate and electrical utility issues, and possibly a disruptive political shift as young people step up.

Once Uranus moves into Gemini in the last week of April, Jupiter will be the only Planet beyond Mars that will change Signs during the year. Jupiter will go from Cancer to Leo by July 1st so expect a year that sets its direction early and stays on course. The old paradigms are quickly falling away in favor of new ideas and innovative actions.

January Forecast

The year starts with Mars, Jupiter and Uranus Retrograde, but a fast Mercury, so at least communications will run smoothly. That Mars in Cancer may cause physical frustrations and by the Full Moon on the 13th that may boil over a bit, so be careful. Jupiter Retrograde in Gemini Square Saturn in Pisces, Conjunct Venus, may cause challenges for the economy. Expect people to be talking about their worries, so give that a pass if you want to avoid the static. **A – 2nd** - Venus enters lovely Pisces, this is a good time to discuss future business and social plans with colleagues and friends. During the month, Venus will cross over Saturn so take your relationships seriously. Those with strong Pisces, prepare to feel attractive and you have permission to be indulgent until February 3rd when Venus enters Aries. **B – 4th** - The Sun and Moon are both making social Aspects today, although with that Moon Conjunct Saturn you may feel the need to keep your emotions in check, and your worries locked away. Great for the Water Signs. **C – 6th** - This is a tumultuous day compounded by an introspective, timid Mars, backing into Cancer so be kind to your body. However, this does signal a good time to go back and finish those home improvement projects. **D – 8th** - Quick moving Mercury enters practical Capricorn, joining the Sun which is Trine the Taurus Moon. A good day for doing practical things with good tasting foods. Have a nice lunch. Good for the Earth Signs. **E – 13th** - The Full Moon on the 13th is complex with Aspects to Mars, Uranus and Neptune, so issues of national or global significance will intrude on people's consciousness. **F – 15th** - Expect a certain amount of chaos and opposition today. Some people may have a hard time speaking their mind and then be subject to outbursts. You Leos behave yourselves! **G – 18th** - The day is filled with positive Aspects, but it will incline people to be serious and considered. This is a good time to initiate projects and move stalled projects along.

H – 19th - The Sun enters Aquarius with a Libra Moon Trine Jupiter in Gemini and Mercury Sextile Venus, so this is a wonderful day for socializing and good conversations. With the Sun joining Pluto there may be a sense of hidden power at this time. *Aquarius, begin counting down to your Solar Return!* **I – 23rd -** There are so many Aspects today, mostly supportive, but some challenging, so expect it to be an eventful day, and take care against overloading your 'to do' list, because there will be distractions. That Sagittarius Moon late in the day helps the Fire Signs be flexible and adjust to all this Air and Water.

J – 26th - This is a practical, social day that could spark some romantic possibilities or creative projects thanks to Venus Sextile Uranus and Mercury Sextile Neptune. Avoid listening to the news too much.

K – 27th - Mercury enters Aquarius joining the Sun, Pluto, and the Asteroid Ceres, so this marks a good time to work with others on projects that benefit the group or wider society. Communication improves and practical changes yield benefits. Good for the Earth Signs.

L – 29th - The New Moon at 9 degrees Aquarius picks up some energy from Jupiter in Gemini, all the Air Signs will feel charged up. Seven of the ten bodies are in either Aquarius or Pisces so there will be a sense at the New Moon that events are wrapping up. See our annual Lunar New Year Forecast online at PlanetaryCalendar.com.

M – 30th - On the day when the world celebrates the Year of the Wood Snake, Uranus turns Direct at 23 degrees Taurus, in a difficult part of the sky. Meanwhile, Jupiter makes an exact Trine with the Sun so there may be a sense of seeing a silver lining behind the dark clouds.

• •

Mercury☿ 20° Sagittarius♐ enters Capricorn♑ on the 8th at 2:29am, enters Aquarius♒ on the 27th at 6:52pm.
Venus♀ 28° Aquarius♒ enters Pisces♓ on the 2nd at 7:23pm.
Mars♂Rx 1° Leo♌ enters Cancer♋ on the 6th at 2:43am.
Jupiter♃Rx 13° Gemini♊. Saturn♄ 14° Pisces♓.
Uranus♅Rx 23° Taurus♉ turns Direct on the 30th at 8:22am at 23° Taurus♉. Neptune♆ 27° Pisces♓. Pluto♇ 1° Aquarius♒.

Signs

♈ Aries Begins
♉ Taurus Owns
♊ Gemini Engages
♋ Cancer Nurtures
♌ Leo Embraces
♍ Virgo Improves
♎ Libra Commits
♏ Scorpio Manages
♐ Sagittarius Views
♑ Capricorn Climbs
♒ Aquarius Herds
♓ Pisces Dreams

Planets

☉ Sun Spirit
☽ Moon Emotes
☿ Mercury Thinks
♀ Venus Feels
♂ Mars Acts
♃ Jupiter Expands
♄ Saturn Contracts
♅ Uranus Disrupts
♆ Neptune Envisions
♇ ⚳ Pluto Unearths

Aspects

☌ Conjunct 0° Aligns
∥ Parallel 0° Equals
✶ Sextile 60° Helps
□ Square 90° Works
△ Trine 120° Supports
☍ Opposition 180° Counters

JANUARY 2025

Sunday	Monday	Tuesday
☾♈ **5** ☌♆☌♂✶☿ 11:00am □☿ 6:29am - 11:00am	♂ Enters ♋ 2:43am 1st Quarter ☽ 3:56pm **B** ☾♈ **6** ✶♃ ☿∥♀ □☿ ☉□☽ Epiphany - 3 King's Day Astrologer's Day	Orthodox Christmas Day △☿✶♀ ☾♉ **7** 2:11pm □♂☌♂☌♇ 1:15pm - 2:11pm
△♀☌♄ ☾♋ **12** ☌△♃ ☍♀	Full ☽ 2:26pm 23°♋ **D** ✶♅☌♂△♆ ☾♋ **13** ☉△♅ ☉☍☽ 8:45pm	Orthodox New Year ✶♃ ☾♌ **14** ♀∥♇ ♀□♃ 1:11am ☍♀ ---------- 1:11am
☉ Enters ♒ 11:59am △♃ **G** ☾♎ **19** ☿✶♀	Martin Luther King Inauguration Day ☾♎ **20** □☿□♂ 8:33pm ----------	3rd Quarter ☽ 12:30pm ☾♏ **21** ☌♂ ☉□☽ 8:19am □♇ 8:19am
I ☾♑ **26** ☿✶♅ ✶♀✶♆ 5:42am □♆ 1:39am - 5:42am	♀ Enters ♒ 6:52pm **J** ☾♑ **27** ✶♄△♅ ☍♂	✶♀✶♆☌♂♂ ☾♒ **28** ✶♀☍♃ 11:31am 7:48am - 11:31am

All calculations are Pacific Clock Time (PST & PDT)

Capricorn the Sea Goat to Aquarius the Water Pourer

Wednesday	Thursday	Friday	Saturday
New Year's Day ☌♇ ☾♒ **1** ☉∥☽ 2:49am ☍♂ ---------- 2:49am	♀ Enters ♓ 7:23pm Chanukah Ends △♃✶☿ ☾♒ **2** ♂☍♇ □♅ 8:12pm ----------	Quadrantid Meteors ☌♀ ☾♓ **3** 7:20am ---------- 7:20am	A ☌♄✶♅ ☾♓ **4** ☉✶♄ ☉✶☽ ☉∥☿ □♃
☿ Enters ♑ 2:29am C ✶♄ ☾♉ **8** ☉△☽	☌♅✶♆✶♂△♇ ☾♊ **9** 5:06pm 2:49pm - 5:06pm	☌♃ ☾♊ **10** □♀□♄	☾♋ **11** 8:23pm □♆ 4:03pm - 8:23pm
E ☾♌ **15** ☉☍♂ □♅ 8:09pm ----------	☾♍ **16** 8:45am ---------- 8:45am	△☿ ☾♍ **17** ☉✶♆ □♃☍♀☍♄	F △♅✶♂△♇ ☾♎ **18** ☿✶♄ ☉△☽ ♀☍♄ 7:32pm ☍♆ 6:01pm - 7:32pm
△♄ ☾♏ **22** ☉∥☽	H △♀✶☿△♂△♆ ☿△♅ ☿∥♇ ☾♐ **23** ♂✶♅ ☿☍♂ 8:28pm ☍♅ 4:03pm - 8:28pm	✶♇ ☾♐ **24** ☉✶☽ ☍♃	☾♐ **25** ♀△♂ ♀∥♆ □♄□♀
New ☽ 4:35am 9°♒ K △♃ ☉∥☽ ☾♒ **29** ☉☌☽	Lunar New Year Year of the Wood Snake L ☉△♃ ☾♓ **30** ♅Dx 2:52pm □♅ 3:28am - 2:52pm	☌♄ ☾♓ **31** □♃	

Add 1 Hour for Mountain Time (MT) Add 2 Hours for Central Time (CT) Add 3 Hours for Eastern Time (ET)

February Forecast

Some of the congestion and frustration of January fades as February progresses. After the 23rd, all the Planets are direct so events and projects will move forward more easily. Only Mercury and Venus change Signs so there isn't too much turbulence. Plus, they both move into Signs that work well in the home life, so this is a good time to improve your close relationships. With four White Circle Days and two Black Box days it's an easy month. Watch out, in the later part of the month Mercury is slowing, preparing to turn Retrograde on March 14th, so those kinds of communication projects will not move forward as easily.

A – 3rd - Venus enters self-focused Aries while Mercury is Trine Jupiter, so communication improves, especially among the Fire Signs. Aries, be prepared to feel attractive and feel free to indulge yourself a bit. Venus is slowing and will turn Retrograde and introverted on April 2nd so artistic projects may slow.

B – 4th - Jupiter turns Direct at 11 degrees Gemini so wherever this is in your chart watch for progress and growth. This should give some help to the economy.

C – 9th - The Sun Conjunct Mercury tends to overload the nervous system and, with Mars, Saturn and Uranus involved, it looks like a very hard-fought Super Bowl.

D – 12th - The Full Moon at 24 degrees Leo and Aquarius is Square Uranus so there may be disruptions to the electrical grid, or some type of extreme weather or geological event. If you have planets Square this opposition, at 24 degrees Fixed, Taurus and Scorpio, you may feel challenged, but take the opportunity to accomplish tasks despite the obstructions.

E – 14th - Mercury enters Pisces on Valentine's Day, an appropriately romantic position. Like Mars in Aries, this is a position that functions best in your homelife because it is sympathetic and dreamy. This is good time for writing, communication and oracles until March 3rd when it enters Aries.

F – 18th - The Sun enters Pisces while the Scorpio Moon makes a Trine to Mercury in Pisces, a wonderfully comfortable day for the Water Signs. *Pisces, begin counting down to your Solar Return!*

G – 20th - That Third Quarter Moon, combined with Mercury Square Jupiter, will make it challenging for the four mutable Signs: Gemini, Virgo, Sagittarius, and Pisces. Those beneficial Lunar Aspects above the date will encourage people to compare themselves to others, which could be good or bad depending on your sense of humor.

H – 23rd – Finally, Mars turns Direct at 17 degrees Cancer so look for where that is in your chart and expect to feel more passionate in that area, especially in the personal aspects of your life. Mars in Cancer is a great time for home improvement projects, until it enters Leo on April 17th.

I – 25th - When Mercury Conjuncts Saturn, spend some time thinking about your spiritual disciplines, whether it is meditation, creating art or playing music. This is a great time to reach out to family members of a different generation, especially between grandkids and grandparents.

J – 27th - The final White Circle Day of the Month on the New Moon finds five Planets and Ceres in Pisces in a loose Square to Jupiter in Gemini and a Trine to Mars in Scorpio. All of this activity can be distracting so remember that the solution to distraction is action.

• •

Mercury☿ 6° Aquarius♒ enters Pisces♓ on the 14th at 4:06am. Venus♀ 27° Pisces♓ enters Aries♈ on the 3rd at 11:56pm. Mars♂ 20° Cancer♋Rx turns Direct on the 23rd at 5:59pm at 17° Cancer♋. Jupiter♃ 11° Gemini♊Rx turns Direct on the 4th at 1:40am 11°♊Gemini. Saturn♄ 17° Pisces♓. Uranus♅ 23° Taurus♉. Neptune♆ 27° Pisces♓. Pluto♇ 2° Aquarius♒.

FEBRUARY 2025

Signs
- ♈ Aries Begins
- ♉ Taurus Owns
- ♊ Gemini Engages
- ♋ Cancer Nurtures
- ♌ Leo Embraces
- ♍ Virgo Improves
- ♎ Libra Commits
- ♏ Scorpio Manages
- ♐ Sagittarius Views
- ♑ Capricorn Climbs
- ♒ Aquarius Herds
- ♓ Pisces Dreams

Planets
- ☉ Sun Spirit
- ☽ Moon Emotes
- ☿ Mercury Thinks
- ♀ Venus Feels
- ♂ Mars Acts
- ♃ Jupiter Expands
- ♄ Saturn Contracts
- ♅ Uranus Disrupts
- ♆ Neptune Envisions
- ♇ Pluto Unearths

Aspects
- ☌ Conjunct 0° Aligns
- ∥ Parallel 0° Equals
- ⚹ Sextile 60° Helps
- □ Square 90° Works
- △ Trine 120° Supports
- ☍ Opposition 180° Counters

Sunday	Monday	Tuesday
Goundhog Day ☽ ♈ 2 ⚹☿⚹♃ ☉⚹☽	♀ Enters ♈ 11:56pm **A** ☽ ♉ **3** 7:33pm □☌♂ □☌♇ ☿△♃ 2:19am – 7:33pm	**B** ☽ ♉ 4 □ ☿ ♃Dx
Super Bowl **C** ☽ ♋ 9 ☌♂△⚹♄⚹♅ ☌♂△♄ ☉☌♀	△♆△♀ ☽ ♌ 10 9:00am ☿□♅ ♂☌♇ 5:09am – 9:00am	⚹♃ ☽ ♌ 11 ☉□♅
☽ ♎ 16 △♃	President's Day ☽ ♏ 17 4:18pm ☉△☽ ☉∥☽ □♀ ♀♇ 3:23pm – 4:18pm	☉ Enters ♓ 2:06am **F** ☽ ♏ 18 △☿
H ☽ ♑ 23 ☉⚹☽ □♀☌♂	♂Dx ⚹☿⚹♄△♅⚹♆ ☽ ♒ 24 9:39pm 7:28pm – 9:39pm	Maha Shivaratri **I** ☽ ♒ 25 ☌♇⚹♀△♃ ☿☌♄

All calculations are Pacific Clock Time (PST & PDT)

Aquarius the Water Pourer to Pisces the Fishes

Wednesday	Thursday	Friday	Saturday
			△♂∗⚷☌♅☌♀∗♇ ☾♈ **1** ♀☌♆ 5:09pm 2:05pm - 5:09pm
1st Quarter ☽ 12:01am ∗♀∗♂☌⚷∗♇ ☾♊ **5** ☉□☽ 10:43pm 7:29pm - 10:43pm	∗♀△♇☌♃ ☾♊ **6**	National Wear Red Day △☿ ☉△♃ ☾♊ **7** ♀∗♇ □♄□♇ 11:51pm	☾♋ **8** △♀ 3:03am ————— 3:03am
Full ☽ 5:53am 24°♌ **D** ☾♍ **12** ☉☌☽ 5:06pm □♅☌♇ 11:11am - 5:06pm	Tu B'Shevat ☾♍ **13** □♃	☿ Enters ♓ 4:06am Valentine's Day **E** ∗♂△♅ ☾♍ **14** ♂☍♄	☾♎ **15** △♇ ☉∥☿ 3:44am ♂♆♂♀ 12:35am - 3:44am
△♂△♅ ☾♏ **19** ♂♅	3rd Quarter ☽ 9:32am **G** △♆∗♇△♀ ☾♐ **20** ☉□☽ 4:54am ♀□♄ 2:05am - 4:54am	☾♐ **21** ♂♃□♇☌♄	☾♑ **22** 3:08pm □♆ 12:38pm - 3:08pm
☾♒ **26** □♅ 2:04pm	New ☽ 4:44pm 9°♓ **J** ☾♓ **27** ☉∥☽ 12:46am ♀∗♇ □♃ ————— 12:46am	△♂☌♄∗♅☌♂ ☾♓ **28** ♀∥♆	

Add 1 Hour for Mountain Time (MT) Add 2 Hours for Central Time (CT) Add 3 Hours for Eastern Time (ET)

March Forecast

THREE BIG EVENTS. A Total Lunar Eclipse on the 13th and a Partial Solar Eclipse on the 29th. Those two weeks in between will be emotionally complex. Neptune enters Aries on the 30th. This Planet associated with gases and chemicals enters the Sign of new beginnings, expect innovation. Neptune moves through Aries over the next fourteen years, expect greater awareness of how household chemicals affect our health, andpersonalized pharmaceuticals. Mercury and Venus turn Retrograde. Personal issues and communication become frustrating. **A – 1st** - Venus turns Retrograde at 10 degrees Aries amid a collection of pleasant Lunar Aspects. When Venus backs up, spend more time for our self-care. On the 27th it backs into Pisces, so people with Sun in Aries will feel special most of the month. **B – 3rd** - A slow moving Mercury enters Aries so wherever this is in your chart, expect delays. **C – 4th** - This is the first of two pleasant White Circle Days. On the 4th the Sun in Pisces Sextile Moon in Taurus includes nice social aspects, great for engaging people, especially Earth and Water Signs. **D – 5th** - A very social day with a Gemini Moon and supportive Lunar Aspects. **E – 12th** - Saturn suppresses the Sun's Solar energy, expect energy levels to feel low. **F – 13th** - The Total Lunar Eclipse at 23 degrees Virgo and Pisces places Saturn Conjunct the Sun, in the Sign when the old season fades into the new Spring. Be careful with your thoughts. Focus on optimism. Some people may be losing hope or wearing down with worry. Herd those you care about towards the future. Mars in Cancer Trine the Sun, and Sextile the Moon, means a good walk, cooking and enjoyable household projects will make all the difference in our mood. For two weeks, people will feel emotionally fragile, be gentle and kind. **G – 14th** - Mercury turns Retrograde at 9 degrees Aries, and will back into Pisces on the 29th before turning Direct on April 7th and getting back on track. **H – 16th** - A Void Of Course all day in Libra will require a good list if you want to get anything done and not wander off course too much.

I – 19th - The Sun Conjunct Neptune and Trine the Moon is a great time to move projects along, especially if it connects with people separated by distances. In other words, do the meeting online.
J – 20th - Welcome to Spring! The first day of Aries sees the Sun entering the Sign near Venus. While there will be some lingering worries, thanks to the Moon in Sagittarius and Jupiter in Gemini, there will be a youthful optimism welling up. *Aries, begin counting down to your Solar Return!* **K – 22nd -** With the Sun Conjunct Venus in Aries and Square the Moon, be careful about being too self-centered and watch out for the narcissists in your life trying to take over your agenda.
L – 24th - This is a very social day with plenty of opportunities for good personal interactions. Although, with Mercury Conjunct the Sun, watch for sensory overload. **M – 27th -** Venus backs into Pisces, the Sign of its Exaltation where it serves so well as the colleague, connecting Aphrodite to Jupiter. This is a good time to contact people related to your work whom you may have forgotten to reconnect with. **N – 28th -** That stack of supportive Lunar Aspects above the Date makes this a thoroughly social day although you may spend the time talking about the Eclipse the next day. **O – 29th -** The Partial Solar Eclipse at 9 degrees Aries coincides with Mercury backing into Pisces, and Neptune entering Aries the next day, so hold onto your smart phone. With Mars and Saturn in feminine (responsive) Signs, we see the growing power of women in significant roles of responsibility. **P – 30th -** Neptune moves into Aries so while this signals the Earth coming into a period of more powerful winds, it also shows growth in new types of fuel.

• •

Mercury☿ 26° Pisces♓ enters Aries♈ on the 3rd at 1:03am at 1° Aries♈, turns Rx on the 14th at 11:45pm, enters Pisces♓ on the 29th at 7:17pm. Venus♀ 10° Aries♈ turns Rx on the 1st at 4:35pm at 10° Aries♈, enters Pisces♓ on the 27th at 1:40am. Mars♂ 17° Cancer♋. Jupiter♃ 12° Gemini♊. Saturn♄ 20° Pisces♓. Uranus♅ 23° Taurus♉.
Neptune♆ 28° Pisces♓ enters Aries♈ on the 30th at 5:00am.
Pluto♇ 2° Aquarius♒.

Signs

♈ Aries Begins
♉ Taurus Owns
♊ Gemini Engages
♋ Cancer Nurtures
♌ Leo Embraces
♍ Virgo Improves
♎ Libra Commits
♏ Scorpio Manages
♐ Sagittarius Views
♑ Capricorn Climbs
♒ Aquarius Herds
♓ Pisces Dreams

Planets

☉ Sun Spirit
☽ Moon Emotes
☿ Mercury Thinks
♀ Venus Feels
♂ Mars Acts
♃ Jupiter Expands
♄ Saturn Contracts
♅ Uranus Disrupts
♆ Neptune Envisions
♇ Pluto Unearths

Aspects

☌ Conjunct 0° Aligns
∥ Parallel 0° Equals
⚹ Sextile 60° Helps
□ Square 90° Works
△ Trine 120° Supports
☍ Opposition 180° Counters

MARCH 2025

Sunday	Monday	Tuesday
♆ Enters ♈ 5:00am **P** ☾♉ **30** 1:15pm □♂□♇ 2:17am - 1:15pm	Eid al-Fitr ☾♉ **31**	
☾♈ **2** ☿♀♆ ☉□♃ □♂ 5:51am	♀ Enters ♈ 1:03am **B** ☾♉ **3** 2:36am □♇ 2:36am	Mardi Gras **C** ⚹♂⚹♄☾♅ ☾♉ **4** ☉⚹♀
Daylight Time Begins ⚹♅△♆ ☾♌ **9** 3:58pm ♂♂ 2:31pm - 3:58pm	△☿△♀⚹♃ ☾♌ **10**	☾♌ **11** ☿♂♀ □♅ 1:15pm
H ☾♎ **16** ☉∥♅♇ □♂ 2:52am	St. Patrick's Day ☾♏ **17** 12:30am □♇ 12:30am	△♀△♄ ☾♏ **18**
⚹♄△♅ ☾♑ **23** ♂♂	⚹♆⚹♀♂♀♇⚹♃ **L** ☉☾♀ ☾♑ **24** ♂♂♂ 8:24am 8:00am - 8:24am	△♃ ☾♒ **25** ♀⚹♇

All calculations are Pacific Clock Time (PST & PDT)

Pisces the Fishes to Aries the Ram

Wednesday	Thursday	Friday	Saturday
			Ramadan Begins **A** ♂♆*♇♂♀*♃ ☾♈ **1** ⋯⋯ 1:51am ♀Rx 12:05am - 1:51am
Ash Wednesday **D** *♆△♇*☿*♀ ☾♊ **5** ☿*♇ 4:29am 2:53am - 4:29am	1st Quarter ☽ 8:31am ☌♃ ☾♊ **6** ☉‖♄ ☉☽ □♄	☾♋ **7** ☉△♂ 8:28am □♆☿ 6:56am - 8:28am	♂♂△♄ ☾♋ **8** ☉△☽ □♀
E ☾♍ **12** ☉♂♄ 12:55am ---- 12:55am	Full ☽ 11:54pm 23°♍ **F** *♂ ☾♍ **13** ☉♂☽ □♃♂♃ Total ☽ Eclipse	Holi - Purim **G** △※△♇ ☉‖☽ ☾♎ **14** ☉*♇ 11:58am ♀ Rx ♂♆ 10:47am - 11:58am	△♃ ☾♎ **15** ♂♀♂☿
I △♆*♇△♀ ☉♂♆ ☾♐ **19** ☉△☽ 1:16pm ♂※ 12:27pm - 1:16pm	☉ Enters ♈ 2:01am **J** △☿ ☾♐ **20** ♂♃ Spring Equinox	☾♐ **21** ♀*♇ □♄□※ 11:52pm ----	3rd Quarter ☽ 4:29am **K** ☾♑ **22** ☉♂♀ 12:28am ☉□☽ □♇□☿ ---- 12:28am
Lailat al-Qadr ☾♓ **26** ⋯⋯ 12:31pm □※ 3:15am - 12:31pm	♀ Enters ♓ 1:40am **M** ☾♓ **27** ☉‖☿ ♀*♇ □♃	**N** △♂♂♄*※♂♀♂♆♀ ☾♈ **28** 1:35pm 1:29pm - 1:35pm	New ☽ 3:57am 9°♈ **O** *♃ ☉♂♆ ☾♈ **29** ☉☽ ☉‖☿ Partial ☉ Eclipse ♀ Enters ♓ 7:17pm

Add 1 Hour for Mountain Time (MT)   Add 2 Hours for Central Time (CT)   Add 3 Hours for Eastern Time (ET)

April Forecast

The first seven days are filled with Aspects with Mercury turning Direct. Communication issues take extra effort. Venus turns Direct on the 12th. All Planets are now moving Direct so projects can be moved along easily. The Full Moon aligns with the Star Spica, from the Virgo, a feminine archetype. Expect women's issues to be highlighted. Near the Taurus Ingress expect those days to be stressful. By the New Moon on the 27th may feel like it is teetering between the past and future. Venus enters Aries on the 30th with a sense of finally moving beyond that.

A – 1st - April Fool's Day is blessed with a stream of supportive Lunar Aspects so there are plenty of opportunities for social and business contacts during the day. There is a Void Of Course Moon in the middle of the day so don't get too distracted. **B – 3rd** - A stack of challenging Lunar Aspects may make today demanding, and another mid-day Void Of Course Moon could be frustrating, so focus on getting the important things done and put off the lightweight stuff for later.

C – 4th - Despite the fact that the Aspects are above the line, they are between some tough characters: Mars, Saturn and Uranus, so expect some radical changes. **D – 5th** - This is a repeat of April 1st with a lineup of supportive, hypersocial Lunar Aspects to the Cancer Moon that command the day. Expect to make a plan for plenty of personal contacts. **E – 6th** - With the Venus Trine Mars and the Aries Sun Sextile Jupiter, this is a great day for a get together, or a one-on-one date, or to launch a new project because you will have the wind at your back.

F – 7th - This is second White Circle Day denoting an abundance supportive Aspects, but the one to pay attention to is Mercury turning Direct at 26 degrees Pisces. It is going to enter Aries on the 15th so wherever that has stalled energy in your chart, it will begin picking up speed. **G – 12th** - This is a powerful Full Moon at 23 degrees Libra, Conjunct the Star Spica, the brightest Star in Virgo, which was known in the pre-Christian era as the Great Goddess of Justice. Spica is a feminine archetype so expect to see issues related to women and their rights in the news. Personally, this is a good time to focus on your self-healing and personal surroundings. Venus turns Direct.

H – 15th - Mercury enters Aries while the Moon is in Martial Scorpio so expect a burst of rambunctious energy today. This is a good time to spark new ideas and projects.   **I – 17th -** Mars enters Leo so hopefully you've gotten the bulk of the home projects done during the Mars in Cancer transit and now it's just painting your colors and enjoying all your hard work. Mars in Leo tends to be dramatic, but generous.

J – 19th - The Sun enters Taurus, leading the other personal Planets. This is when the leaves fill out. On the 20th the Sun will Square Mars in Leo. Look at where Taurus and Leo are in your chart because there may be tension between those parts of your life, which can be resolved with productive actions. *Taurus, begin counting down to your Solar Return!* **K – 20th -** The day is packed with so many Lunar and Planetary Aspects that everyone is going to be feeling a little tuned up, so take it slowly and gracefully.   **L – 24th -** A group of exciting Lunar Aspects coupled with Venus Conjunct Saturn makes this a good time to meet new people and forge relationships based on shared beliefs.

M – 26th - An all-day long Void Of Course Moon in Aries could see this day disappear into distractions. Make a good task list.

N – 27th - The New Moon at 7 degrees Taurus, while Mars is in early Taurus, may feel like a cow in a China shop. Tempers may clash with stubbornness so stay on your toes.   **O – 30th -** Venus enters Aries, expect people to be more self-aware and focused on their own concerns.

• •

Mercury☿Rx 28° Pisces♓ turns Direct on the 7th at 4:07am at 24° Pisces♓, enters Aries♈ on the 15th at 11:24pm. Venus♀Rx 27° Pisces♓ turns Direct on the 12th at 6:02pm at 24° Pisces♓, enters Aries♈ on the 30th at 10:15am. Mars♂ 23° Cancer♋, enters Leo♌ on the 17th at 9:20pm. Jupiter♃ 16° Gemini♊. Saturn♄ 24° Pisces♓. Uranus♅ 24° Taurus♉. Neptune♆ 00° Aries♈. Pluto♇ 3° Aquarius♒.

Signs

- ♈ Aries Begins
- ♉ Taurus Owns
- ♊ Gemini Engages
- ♋ Cancer Nurtures
- ♌ Leo Embraces
- ♍ Virgo Improves
- ♎ Libra Commits
- ♏ Scorpio Manages
- ♐ Sagittarius Views
- ♑ Capricorn Climbs
- ♒ Aquarius Herds
- ♓ Pisces Dreams

Planets

- ☉ Sun Spirit
- ☽ Moon Emotes
- ☿ Mercury Thinks
- ♀ Venus Feels
- ♂ Mars Acts
- ♃ Jupiter Expands
- ♄ Saturn Contracts
- ♅ Uranus Disrupts
- ♆ Neptune Envisions
- ♇ **Pluto Unearths**

Aspects

- ☌ Conjunct 0° Aligns
- ∥ Parallel 0° Equals
- ✶ Sextile 60° Helps
- □ Square 90° Works
- △ Trine 120° Supports
- ☍ Opposition 180° Counters

APRIL 2025

Sunday	Monday	Tuesday
		A "April Fools Day" ✶♂✶♄☌♅✶♀✶♇△♆ ☽♊ 1 1:25pm 10:42am - 1:25pm
E ☽♌ 6 ♀△♂ ☉✶♃ ♂☌♇ 9:08pm	**F** ☽♌ 7 ✶♃ ♀✶♅ ☉☽ ♀Dx □♅	☽♍ 8 6:39am 6:39am
Passover Begins Palm Sunday ☽♏ 13 6:53am □♂☌♀ 3:00am - 6:53am	☽♏ 14	♀ Enters ♈ 11:24pm **H** ☌♀△♄☌♂△♀△♅ ☽♐ 15 7:36pm ♂∥♃ ♂✶♓ Tax Day 7:23pm - 7:36pm
3rd Quarter ☽ 6:35pm Easter - Orthodox Easter **K** ✶♀△♅✶♄✶♆☌♇△♆ ☽♒ 20 4:21pm ☌♂ Passover Ends 10:20am - 4:21pm	Easter Monday Orthodox Easter Monday Boston Marathon ☽♒ 21	Lyrid Meteors Peak Earth Day △♃ ☽♓ 22 10:06pm □♅ 2:55pm - 10:06pm
New ☽ 12:30pm 7° ♉ **N** ☽♉ 27 ☉☌☽ 12:16am □♇☌♂ ------12:16am	♂✶♅✶♄✶♇ ☽♊ 28 11:34pm 10:17pm - 11:34pm	✶♆△♇✶♂✶♀ ☽♊ 29

All calculations are Pacific Clock Time (PST & PDT)

Aries the Ram to Taurus the Bull

Wednesday	Thursday	Friday	Saturday
☾ ♊ 2 ♂♃ ☉✳☽ ☉∥♀	**B** ☾ ♋ **3** 3:49pm □♄□♀☿♆ 11:26am - 3:49pm	1st Quarter ☽ 7:14pm **C** ☾ ♋ 4 ♂△♄ ♂✳♅ ♄✳♅ ☉□☽	**D** ☾ ♌ 5 9:33pm ✳♅△♄♂♂△♀△♀△♃ 3:54pm - 9:33pm
☾ ♍ 9 □♃	☾ ♎ 10 6:11pm ♂♀♂♄♂♀♂♆ △♅✳♂ 12:48pm - 6:11pm	☾ ♎ 11 △♀	Full ☽ 5:22pm 23° ♎ **G** ☾ ♎ 12 △♃ ♀Dx ♂♂☽
☾ ♐ 16 ✳♀ ☿♂♆	♂ Enters ♌ 9:20pm **I** ☾ ♐ 17 ♂♃□♀	Good Friday Orthodox Good Friday ☾ ♑ 18 7:11am □♄□♆□♀ ☉△☽ 4:37am - 7:11am	☉ Enters ♉ 12:55pm **J** ☾ ♑ 19 ♂△♆
Lyrid Meteors Peak Yom HaShoah ☾ ♓ 23 ☉✳☽ ☉□♀	**L** ☾ ♓ **24** 7:57pm ✳♅♂♄♂♀ ♀♂♄ □♃	♂♆△♂✳♀♂♀ ☾ ♈ 25 12:23am ☿∥♀	**M** ☾ ♈ **26** 9:17am ✳♃ ☉∥☽ ♂♂♀
♀ Enters ♈ 10:15am **O** ☾ ♊ 30 9:48pm ♂♃ □♄			

Add 1 Hour for Mountain Time (MT)   Add 2 Hours for Central Time (CT)   Add 3 Hours for Eastern Time (ET)

May Forecast

The big event this month is Saturn entering Aries on the 24th. In this position there is a tendency to challenge authority, and that results in martyrs being created. The Saturn cycle is 28 years so, in pre-modern times, that was seen as not only the marker of maturity, but often the marker of old age. That's why Saturn has been connected to Father Time. Despite the fact that Astrologers in the 1930's made Capricorn its sole Ruled Sign, in reality, it is equally related to Aquarius and leans towards the masculine there. In Aries, Saturn will challenge the old, conservative structures of Capricorn and Cancer, and encourage the technological innovators of Aquarius and Leo. The other big event is Pluto turning Retrograde in Aquarius on the 4th. Before this, all the Planets were moving Direct which encourages progress, so this is the first, subtle hint of slowing. But it's not until July that other Planets begin turning Retrograde and the pace slows significantly and rapid progress will be harder to achieve.

A – 4th - When Pluto turns Retrograde at 3 degrees Aquarius it won't have an obvious effect, but there will be the first, smallest hints of progress slowing down. **B – 6th -** This is a well-organized day for accomplishing tasks but don't let the desire for perfect get in the way of the good. **C – 10th -** Mercury entering stable, patient Taurus is a good reminder to slow down and take more time enjoying the people around you. This is good for gardening and cooking.

D – 12th - The Full Moon at 22 degrees Scorpio and Taurus happens amid loose aspects with Saturn and Uranus. Meanwhile Mercury is Square Pluto, so there will be some odd tensions around it. People in committed relationships should tip their toe for a few days to avoid arguments. Look where this fits in your chart because Taurus, Leo, Scorpio and Aquarius will feel this the most.

E – 17th - This is a lively day with the Sun Trine Moon after the Full Moon, which is usually a good time to accomplish tasks. But be careful because the Sun is Conjunct Uranus and Mercury is Square Mars so people may be prone to accidents and unexpected complications.

F – 20th - The Sun enters Gemini, Square the Moon and Sextile Saturn, so there will be a serious tone to the Sun's Ingress. But hope springs eternal, because the Sun is joining Jupiter in Gemini, so the Air Signs will feel empowered. *Gemini, begin counting down to your Solar Return!* **G – 22nd -** With Venus Trine Mars and the Sun Sextile the Moon, the relationship between the polarities will be smooth and, with so many social Aspects to the Moon, it can be a lovely day as long as you get out and see people. Great for the Fire Signs.

H – 24th - Saturn enters Aries, a deeply personal position, and it will be there for the next couple of years. Being Square the USA's Sun position and opposite its founding Saturn in Libra, this transit is not an easy time in the USA, but great things can be accomplished. The Ingress happens on the same day that Mercury and Uranus are Conjunct and Parallel, so expect intense messages from Mother Earth about our climate, nature and youth. **I – 25th -** Mercury enters witty and mischievous Gemini, so conversation as an art will shine and this is especially good for business. Mercury remains there until the 8th of June. **J – 26th -** This New Moon at 6 degrees of Gemini is concentrated in Air and Fire Signs, so expect lots of activity and potential discord. Although this is a great time for flirting and moving potential relationships along. This White Circle notes an especially social Memorial Day. **K – 27th -** This White Circle is an easy day to connect with others. **L – 29th -** When the Sun Conjuncts Mercury, watch out for moving a little too fast for your own good.

• •

Mercury☿ 15° Aries♈ enters Taurus♉ on the 10th at 5:14am, enters Gemini♊ on the 25th at 5:59pm. Venus♀ 0° Aries♈. Mars♂ 5° Leo♌. Jupiter♃ 21° Gemini♊. Saturn♄ 27° Pisces♓ enters Aries♈ on the 24th at 8:35pm. Uranus♅ 26° Taurus♉. Neptune♆ 01° Aries♈. Pluto♇ 3° Aquarius♒ turns Rx on the 4th at 8:27am at 3° Aquarius♒.

Signs

♈ Aries Begins
♉ Taurus Owns
♊ Gemini Engages
♋ Cancer Nurtures
♌ Leo Embraces
♍ Virgo Improves
♎ Libra Commits
♏ Scorpio Manages
♐ Sagittarius Views
♑ Capricorn Climbs
♒ Aquarius Herds
♓ Pisces Dreams

Planets

☉ Sun Spirit
☽ Moon Emotes
☿ Mercury Thinks
♀ Venus Feels
♂ Mars Acts
♃ Jupiter Expands
♄ Saturn Contracts
♅ Uranus Disrupts
♆ Neptune Envisions
♇ ♇ Pluto Unearths

Aspects

☌ Conjunct 0° Aligns
∥ Parallel 0° Equals
✶ Sextile 60° Helps
□ Square 90° Works
△ Trine 120° Supports
☍ Opposition 180° Counters

MAY 2025

Sunday	Monday	Tuesday
1st Quarter ☽ 6:51am **A** ☾♌ **4** △☿✶♃ ☉□☽ ♀Rx	Cinco de Mayo Eta Aquarid Meteors ☾♍ **5** ☿✶♃ ☉∥☽ □♅ 12:39pm 6:03am - 12:39pm	**B** ☾♍ **6** ☉△☽ ♀∥♆
Mother's Day ☾♏ **11** ♂∥♅ □♂	Full ☽ 9:55am 22° ♏ △♄ ☾♏ **12** ☉☍☽ ☿♇ ♂☍♇ 11:36pm ----	△♆✶♇△♀ ☾♐ **13** 1:34am ---- 1:34am
✶♆☌♇✶♀ ☾♒ **18**	△♃ ☾♒ **19** ♂☌☿	☉ Enters ♊ 11:54am 3rd Quarter ☽ 4:58am **F** ☾♓ **20** ☉✶♄ ☉∥☽ 5:28am □♅ 4:58am - 5:28am
☿ Enters ♊ 5:59pm **I** ☾♉ **25** ☿✶♄ ☉∥☽ □♂	New ☽ 8:02pm 6° ♊ **J** ☌♅✶♄☌☿✶♆△♀ ☾♊ **26** ☉☌☽ ☉✶♆ 10:21am Memorial Day 6:51am - 10:21am	**K** ✶♂✶♀ ☾♊ **27** ♀△♇

All calculations are Pacific Clock Time (PST & PDT)

Taurus the Bull to Gemini the Twins

Wednesday	Thursday	Friday	Saturday
	May Day / Lei Day ☾♋ 1 ☉✶☽ 12:22am □♀□♆ ---------- 12:22am	Yom Ha'atzmaut Evening ✶♅ ☾♋ 2 ♀☌♆ □☿	Kentucky Derby △♄△♆△♀☌♂ ☾♌ 3 4:28am ☍♇ 1:01am - 4:28am
△♅ ☾♍ 7 □♃☍♄ 9:10pm ----------	△♇✶♂ ☾♎ 8 12:06am ☍♆☍♀ ---------- 12:06am	△♃ ☾♎ 9 11:17pm ----------	☿ Enters ♉ 5:14am C ☾♏ 10 12:58pm ☍☿□♇ ---------- 12:58pm
△♂ ☾♐ 14 ☉∥♂	☾♑ 15 12:57pm ☍♃□♄△♆ 11:28am - 12:57pm	Lag BaOmer △☿ ☾♑ 16 ☉∥♅ □♀	Armed Forces Day E △♅✶♄ ☾♒ 17 ☉△☽ ☉☌♅ ☿□♂ 10:29pm 9:26pm - 10:29pm
✶☿ ☾♓ 21	✶♅☌♄☌♆✶♇ G ☾♈ 22 ☉✶☽ ☉✶♆ ☿∥♂ ♀△♂ 9:25am □♃ 9:06am - 9:25am	△♂☌♀ ☾♈ 23	♄ Enters ♈ 8:35pm H ✶♃ ☾♉ 24 ☿∥♅ ☿☌♅ ☉△♇ 10:37am □♇ 4:43am - 10:37am
☌♃ ☾♋ 28 ☉∥☿ 10:32am □♄□♆ 6:00am - 10:32am	L ☾♋ 29 ☉☌☿	✶♅△♄△♆ ☾♌ 30 1:16pm □♀☍♇ 9:50am - 1:16pm	✶☿ ☾♌ 31 ☿∥♃ ☉✶☽ ☉∥☽

Add 1 Hour for Mountain Time (MT) Add 2 Hours for Central Time (CT) Add 3 Hours for Eastern Time (ET)

June Forecast

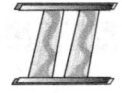

This month has two significant events. Jupiter enters its Exalted Sign Cancer, issues related to women and the home will see the benefits. Jupiter Square Saturn is harder on the economy, but offers ideas about working with our families at home to create personal improvements. Jupiter will turn Retrograde on November 11th. Where Jupiter is moving in your chart wants to expand. Heads up Cancer Natives, Jupiter Transits are fun but watch out for overdoing things in terms of food and exercise. The other big event is the Summer Solstice when the Sun enters Cancer. Historically, the Sun ruled Leo and Cancer, and the Sign of the Crab was the image that described women as leaders. Why? Because this time year, while the men were hunting, the women would lead the tribe and the children to the cool shorelines to hunt crabs and the roast them on fires made from driftwood. **A – 5th -** Venus enters Taurus. It's a lovely social position on the same day that Mercury Sextiles Mars and the Sun Trines the Moon, so there will be a sense of wellbeing and everything being in order. Venus will spend a month in Taurus, so this is a good time to focus on the earthy things that make your life more pleasurable.

B – 8th - A fast moving Mercury enters Cancer the day before Jupiter joins it, so ideas and communications are moving quickly. This is a great time for writing projects and working on your nest egg.

9th - A fast moving Jupiter enters its Exalted Sign of Cancer, so look for that in your chart because there are possibilities waiting for you in that part of your life. This is great for the Water Signs, although the Cancerians may find dealing with this much attention challenging.

D – 11th - Even though the Sun is in Gemini, an Air Sign, this chart is all about Earth, Water and Fire, including that Sagittarius Full Moon at 20 degrees being supported by Mars in Leo. Don't be surprised if people are impetuous and it may be difficult to get much accomplished between now and the New Moon.

E – 15th - We wish we could make Father's Day a little more pleasant, but with Saturn in Aries Square Jupiter in Cancer, the best thing to do is whatever Mom suggests. **F – 17th -** Mars enters detail focused Virgo, where it will be there until August 6th, and it's moving quickly. That makes it a good time to help those organizations you belong to, as well as attending to health issues you've ignored. **G – 20th -** The Sun enters Cancer at the Summer Solstice, the longest few days of the year. Mercury Square the Moon happens early in the day, but supportive Mars and Jupiter Aspects happen later when the Moon enters Taurus. The highlight is when the Sun joins Jupiter in Cancer. This is one of the best times to travel to someplace cool with people you care about. *Cancerians, begin counting down to your Solar Return!*

H – 23rd - The Gemini Moon Square the Virgo Mars may make you want to rush projects that really need more time. The day long Void Of Course Moon just complicates that by making it hard to stay on track. Make a list of what you want to accomplish. **I – 24th -** This exceptionally long Void Of Course stretches over two full days, but at least today, the Sun and Jupiter are Conjunct. This is symbolic of the King visiting the Duchess at her estate. So, you may be busy reacting today, instead of acting. **J – 25th –** Finally, after that very distracted Full Moon, and distracting Void Of Course with the Jupiter Sun Conjunction, this New Moon at 4 degrees Cancer is all about getting things done. So, get your tools in order. **K – 26th -** Mercury Sextiles Uranus setting off information sparks, and then enters dramatic Leo, while the Sun in Cancer Sextiles Mars bringing energy to physical tasks. But Mercury is slowing so short distance travel and communication issues are too. Mercury will turn Retrograde on the 17th of July.

• •

Mercury☿ 13° GeminiⅡ enters Cancer♋ on the 8th at 3:57pm, enters Leo♌ on the 26th at 2:08pm. Venus♀ 25° Aries♈ enters Taurus♉ on the 5th at 9:42pm. Mars♂ 21° Leo♌ enters Virgo♍ on the 17th at 1:35am. Jupiter♃ 28° GeminiⅡ enters Cancer♋ on the 9th at 2:01pm. Saturn♄ 0° Aries♈. Uranus♅ 28° Taurus♉. Neptune♆ 01° Aries♈. Pluto♇ Rx 3° Aquarius♒.

Signs

♈ Aries Begins
♉ Taurus Owns
♊ Gemini Engages
♋ Cancer Nurtures
♌ Leo Embraces
♍ Virgo Improves
♎ Libra Commits
♏ Scorpio Manages
♐ Sagittarius Views
♑ Capricorn Climbs
♒ Aquarius Herds
♓ Pisces Dreams

Planets

☉ Sun Spirit
☽ Moon Emotes
☿ Mercury Thinks
♀ Venus Feels
♂ Mars Acts
♃ Jupiter Expands
♄ Saturn Contracts
♅ Uranus Disrupts
♆ Neptune Envisions
♇ ♇ Pluto Unearths

Aspects

☌ Conjunct 0° Aligns
∥ Parallel 0° Equals
✶ Sextile 60° Helps
□ Square 90° Works
△ Trine 120° Supports
☍ Opposition 180° Counters

JUNE 2025

Sunday	Monday	Tuesday
Pride Month ♂♂△♀✶♃ ☾ ♍ **1** 7:59pm □♅ 4:37pm - 7:59pm	1st Quarter ☽ Shavuot ☾ ♍ **2** ☉□☽	☾ ♍ **3** □☿
♀ Enters ♋ 3:57pm **B** ☾ ♏ **8** ☿△♃ □♂	♃ Enters ♋ 2:01pm **C** △♄△✶♀✶♆ ☾ **9** ♀□♄ 7:55am ☍♅ ♀□♇ ☿△♇ 5:06am - 7:55am	☾ ♐ **10**
Father's Day **E** ☾ ♒ **15** ☌♇□♅ ♃□♄	△♃ ♀∥♂ ☾ ♓ **16** ☉△☽ 11:08am □♅☌♂ 10:30am - 11:08am	♂ Enters ♍ 1:35am **F** ✶♀△✶ ☾ ♓ **17**
✶☿♅✶♄□♆ ☾ ♊ **22** ☿☌♃ 7:56pm ☉□♄ 6:50pm - 7:56pm	**H** △♇ ☾ ♊ **23** ☉□♆ □♂ 1:25am	**I** ☾ ♋ **24** ☌♃ 8:43pm □♄ 8:43pm
✶♃☌♂ ♀∥♅ ☾ ♍ **29** ☉✶♇ 4:43am ♀☌♇ □♅ 4:02am - 4:43am	☾ ♍ **30**	

All calculations are Pacific Clock Time (PST & PDT)

Gemini the Twins to Cancer the Crab

Wednesday	Thursday	Friday	Saturday
△⚥△♇ ☾ ♎ **4** 6:38am ♀✶♃ ♂☌♄☌♅☌♆ 4:11am - 6:38am	♀ Enters ♉ 9:42pm **A** ☾ ♎ **5** ☿✶♂ ☉△☽	✶♂△♀△♃ ☾ ♏ **6** 7:22pm ☍♀ 6:04pm - 7:22pm	Eid al-Adha ☾ ♏ **7** □♇
Full ☽ 12:43am 20° Kamehameha Day **D** ☾ ♑ **11** 6:54pm ♂☌♄□♀ 12:57pm - 6:54pm	△♂ ☾ ♑ **12** ☿✶♀ ☉☌☽ ☍☿	△♀ ☾ ♑ **13**	Flag Day △⚥✶♄✶♆☌♀ ☾ ♒ **14** 3:59am □♀ 1:51am - 3:59am	☉‖♃
3rd Quarter ☽ 12:18pm ✶⚥☌♄☌♆☌♀ ☾ ♈ **18** 4:07pm □♃ ♄□♆ 2:34pm - 4:07pm	Juneteenth ☾ ♈ **19**	☉ Enters ♋ 7:42pm **G** △♂✶♃ ☉‖☿ ☾ ♉ **20** 6:52pm ☉✶☽ □☿ Summer Solstice 6:49pm - 6:52pm	☍♀ ☾ ♉ **21** ☿‖♃ □♀
New ☽ 3:31am 4° ♋ **J** ♂✶♂ ☾ ♋ **25** ☉☌☽ □♆	♀ Enters ♌ 12:08pm **K** ✶♀✶♅ ☾ ♌ **26** ☉✶♂ 11:05pm ☿✶♅ 10:15pm - 11:05pm	Muharram ♂♀△♄△♆ ☿△♄ ☾ ♌ **27** ☉‖☽ ☍♀	☉‖♃ ☾ ♌ **28** ☿△♆ □♀

Add 1 Hour for Mountain Time (MT) Add 2 Hours for Central Time (CT) Add 3 Hours for Eastern Time (ET)

July Forecast

An eventful month. Mercury, Neptune and Saturn turn Retrograde, so politics and commerce slow down. Venus is moving fast, so your personal affairs have the wind in their sails. *Big event: Uranus enters Gemini on the 7th.* This is the USA's natal position. The previous time it was in Gemini was at the start of World War II, before that the American Civil War, before that was during the Revolutionary War. *It Retrogrades back into Taurus on November 7th, returns to Gemini in May 2026 until May of 2033.* Clearly the battle for democracy is on. The day before Uranus entered Gemini, women became official members of the USA military for the first time. In the middle of the transit, large numbers of refugees were relocating, and the state of Israel was founded. *Uranus is not a Planet that you want to ignore.* **A – 2nd** - The day starts easily except for the Void Of Course Moon that starts after lunch which could leave you open to distractions. **B – 3rd** - This whole day has a Void Of Course Moon. As Planets come to the angles, there will be periodic episodes of being focused, interspersed with some wandering attention so have a good list and visual cues about what you want to accomplish.

C – 4th - On Independence Day, a fast Venus enters Gemini, a position that thrives on good conversation and clever flirting. Neptune turns Retrograde at 2 degrees Aries, so as more outer Planets turn Retrograde, outer world events slow down. July 4th is the USA's Solar Return when the Sun Returns to the same Degree when the USA was founded. Interestingly, on this day, Jupiter has returned to the same degree where it was on July 4th, 1776, at five degrees Cancer. So, expect big things this year. It may not be easy, but it is going to be exciting. The Solar Return Moon is in Scorpio, or more properly called, the Eagle, the Feminine Ruling Sign of Mars, women weill be very prominent in American politics this year. **D – 5th** - This is a nice, easy, emotional Saturday with that White Circle and the Sun Trine the Scorpio Moon.

E — 7th - Boom! Uranus enters Gemini, the Sign it was in when the USA was founded, adding to the excitement and sizzle in politics this year. **F — 8th -** This is another extended Void Of Course Moon so we suggest you make a list, especially with that Sagittarius Moon, since they are inclined to be easily distracted. **G — 9th -** With those challenging Lunar Aspects, count on people around you to expect a lot from you today. **H — 10th -** On this Full Moon, at 18 degrees Capricorn and Cancer, when you feel challenged, focus on the things you can control. It is going to be the little things where you will see progress. Look for where this is taking place in your chart because those areas will require some emotional discipline. **I — 12th -** Saturn turns Retrograde at 1 degree Aries, which is a point with tremendous leverage, so expect some cultural shifts. **J — 13th -** Another long Void Of Course Moon in Aquarius could make it hard to stay focused, except on social media. **K — 17th -** A slowing Mercury turns Retrograde at 15 degrees Leo so watch for where that happens in your chart. **L — 18th -** This White Circle is due to a lovely Taurus Moon, making a friendly Sextile to Jupiter, newly in Cancer, the Moon's Ruler. Meanwhile Mercury is in Leo, Sextile flirty Venus in Gemini, so it makes a pleasant day with easy and fun communication. **M — 22nd -** The Sun enters Leo, warming up the Charts, with the Moon in Cancer, so both are in Ruling Signs for a good couple of days to be out there in the world. *Leos, begin counting down to your Solar Return!* **N — 24th -** The New Moon at 2 degrees Leo is cooperative rather than dynamic, so we come into the high summer with the need to attend to the simple things, and let the big stuff wait. **O — 30th -** Venus enters homey Cancer on a day when the Moon is Void Of Course in Libra all day. **P — 31st -** Mercury Retrograde is Conjunct the Sun so don't be surprised if you feel overwhelmed.

• •

Mercury☿ 5° Leo♌ turns Rx on the 17th at 9:44pm at 15° Leo♌. Venus♀ 26° Taurus♉ enters Gemini♊ on the 4th at 8:30am, enters Cancer♋ on the 30th at 8:56pm. Mars♂ 7° Virgo♍. Jupiter♃ 4° Cancer♋. Saturn♄ 1° Aries♈ turns Rx on the 12th at 9:07pm at 1° Aries♈. Uranus♅ 29° Taurus♉ enters Gemini♊ on the 7th at 12:45am. Neptune♆ 02° Aries♈ turns Rx on the 4th at 2:32pm at 02° Aries♈. Pluto♇ Rx 3° Aquarius♒.

Signs

♈ Aries Begins
♉ Taurus Owns
♊ Gemini Engages
♋ Cancer Nurtures
♌ Leo Embraces
♍ Virgo Improves
♎ Libra Commits
♏ Scorpio Manages
♐ Sagittarius Views
♑ Capricorn Climbs
♒ Aquarius Herds
♓ Pisces Dreams

Planets

☉ Sun Spirit
☽ Moon Emotes
☿ Mercury Thinks
♀ Venus Feels
♂ Mars Acts
♃ Jupiter Expands
♄ Saturn Contracts
♅ Uranus Disrupts
♆ Neptune Envisions
♇ ⚥ Pluto Unearths

Aspects

☌ Conjunct 0° Aligns
∥ Parallel 0° Equals
✶ Sextile 60° Helps
□ Square 90° Works
△ Trine 120° Supports
☍ Opposition 180° Counters

JULY 2025

Sunday	Monday	Tuesday
		△♀△♅△♇ ☾ ♎ **1** 2:16pm ☍♄☍♆ 1:46pm - 2:16pm
Ashura △♄△♆✶♃ ♀✶♅ ☾ ♐ **6** ♀✶♄ 3:05pm ☌♅☍♀ 3:03pm - 3:05pm	♅ Enters ♊ 12:45am **E** △♀ ☾ ♐ **7** ♀△♇ □♂ 2:29pm	**F** ☾ ♐ **8**
	Bastille Day	
J ☾ ♓ **13** 4:44pm □♅ ---- 4:44pm	☾ ♓ **14** △♃ □♀☍♂ 12:51pm ----	✶♅ ☉△☽ ☾ ♈ **15** ♀∥♅ 9:32pm 10:09am - 9:32pm
☌♅✶♄✶♆△♇ ☾ ♊ **20** 3:21am ---- 3:21am	✶☿☌♇ ☾ ♊ **21** □♂	☉ Enters ♌ 6:29am **M** ☌♃ ☉✶♅ ☾ ♋ **22** ☉∥♅ 5:25am □♄□♀ ---- 5:25am
✶♃ ☾ ♍ **27**	Delta Aquarid Meteors ☌♂ ☾ ♎ **28** 10:42pm □♀ 5:56pm - 10:42pm	Delta Aquarid Meteors △♅△♀✶♃ ☾ ♎ **29** ☉✶☽ ☍♄☍♆♃ 8:58pm ----

All calculations are Pacific Clock Time (PST & PDT)

48

Cancer the Crab to Leo the Lion

Wednesday	Thursday	Friday	Saturday
1st Quarter ☽ 12:29pm **A** ☾♎ *☿ **2** □♃ ---- 12:29pm ----	**B** ☾♎ **3**	♀ Enters ♊ 8:30am Independence Day **C** ☾♏ △♃*♂ ☿‖♀ **4** ☉♂♀ 2:32am ♇Rx □♇♀ ---- 2:32am ----	**D** ☾♏ **5** ☉△☽
G ☾♑ **9** 1:54am □♃☉♇♀♃ ---- 1:54am ----	Full ☽ 1:36pm 18° ♑ **H** ☾♑ △♂ **10** ☉♂☽ ---- 1:36pm ----	△⚴*♄*♆♂♀ **C** ☾♒ **11** 10:20am ---- 10:20am ----	**I** ☾♒ △♀ **12** ♄Rx ♂♀ 12:44pm
J ☾♈ ♂♄☉♆*♀♀ **16** □♃	3rd Quarter ☽ 5:37pm **K** ☾♈ △☿ **17** ☉□☽ ☿Rx ---- 5:37pm ----	**L** ☾♉ *♃ **18** ☿*♀ 12:58am □♇ ---- 12:58am ----	**M** ☾♉ △♂ ☉*☽ **19** ☉‖♀ □☿ ☉‖☽ 11:43pm
M ☾♋ *♂ **23** ♀□♂ 5:41pm ----	New ☽ 12:10pm 2° ♌ **N** ☾♌ *⚴△♄△♆ **24** ☉♂☽ 8:28am ☉△♀ ☉△♄ ♂♀ ☉♂♀ ---- 8:28am ----	**C** ☾♌ ♂☿ **25** ☉‖☽	**C** ☾♍ *♀ **26** 1:55pm □⚴ 4:01am - 1:55pm
♀ Enters ♋ 8:56pm **O** ☾♎ **30**	**P** ☾♏ △♀ **31** ☉♂♀ 10:24am □♇ ---- 10:24am ----		

Add 1 Hour for Mountain Time (MT) Add 2 Hours for Central Time (CT) Add 3 Hours for Eastern Time (ET)

August Forecast

Astrologically this is a less complicated month, with most of the changes happening among the personal Planets, so be prepared to change your goals and directions and move onto the next stage. Mercury turning Direct on the 11th should smooth the waters although, be prepared for that New Moon on the 22nd, the day the Sun enters Virgo. This is the position of the star Regulus, the heart of the Lion. We point this out every year because it gives this period a lovely glow you should take the time to enjoy. As its position has moved from Tropical Leo into Tropical Virgo, better known as the Great Goddess, it is empowering the feminine, and this Lunation is all about that. Venus and Jupiter are in Cancer, the Sign of feminine Leadership. Mars is in the deeply personal position of Libra, the masculine Sign of Venus, that works especially well in home life. Meanwhile, the Asteroids Vesta and Juno, the flame and the wife of Jupiter, are exactly Conjunct at 20 degrees Scorpio, the feminine Sign of Mars and a spot known for mental brilliance. The theme we see at this year of powerful women acting decisively at critical times continues this month. Virgo was originally called the Great Goddess because this was the time of year when the women would harvest the plants, most notably the grapes to make wine. The Constellation is the largest on the Ecliptic. She holds grapes in her left hand and a spike, or knife, for trimming the grapes in her right hand. The early Christian Astrologers wanted to destroy the Goddess' temples so they changed her knife into a stalk of wheat. They rebranded the Goddess, who was an artisan farmer and winemaker, into a helpless Virgin. But she is really the Goddess of Justice! **A – 1st –** August starts with a Black Box due to a lineup of Planetary Squares including the Sun, Moon, Venus, Saturn and Neptune. Saturn and Neptune, being located so close together and Retrograde, complicates this day. There may be some inter-generational conflicts, or arguments over money so tread lightly.

B – 3rd - That Sagittarius Moon triggers a series of energizing aspects so take advantage of this social, optimistic day.

C – 6th - Mars enters Libra, a position that may require patience, and it will be there until November 22nd so get used to carefully considered decisions before actions are taken. An almost day long Void Of Course Moon in Capricorn may be a bit frustrating.

D – 7th - The day long Void Of Course Moon in Capricorn finally ends with the Moon entering Aquarius late in the day, so a good list of tasks is helpful. Especially because a lineup of Lunar Aspects, including to the Outer Planets, can divert your attention to the news 'out there' a little too much. **E – 8th & 9th -** This Full Moon may be emotionally difficult, partly because a Mars Saturn opposition can put people at loggerheads. With Jupiter at the Star Sirius and so close to Venus, find ways to finesse the issues by using your emotional intelligence.

F – 11th - Mercury turns Direct at 4 degrees Leo so things like communications, phones, computers will start behaving better. Between the 11th and the 22nd things calm down. **G – 22nd -** The Sun enters Virgo at the New Moon at zero degrees Virgo, Conjunct the Star Regulus, the heart of the Lion. This is a powerful set point that speaks about the power of the Goddess. The pre-Christian name of the Sign was the Great Goddess of Justice, and it celebrated her talents as a farmer and winemaker. In the Constellation, the Goddess holds a bunch of grapes in her left hand and a work knife in her right. *Virgos, begin the countdown to your Solar Return!* **H – 25th -** Venus enters big hearted Leo so if that is your Sun, Moon or Rising Sign prepare to feel attractive and deserving of being indulged until the 19th of September.

I – 27th - Another day-long Void Of Course Moon in Libra may make it hard to stay on track so have a good list and some visual clues.

• •

Mercury☿Rx 8° Leo♌ turns Direct on the 11th at 12:29am at 4° Leo♌. Venus♀ 1° Cancer♋ enters Leo♌ on the 25th at 9:26am. Mars♂ 26° Virgo♍ enters Libra♎ on the 6th at 4:23pm. Jupiter♃ 11° Cancer♋. Saturn♄Rx 1° Aries♈. Uranus♅ 0° Gemini♊. Neptune♆ Rx 1° Aries♈. Pluto♇ Rx 2° Aquarius♒.

Signs

♈ Aries Begins
♉ Taurus Owns
♊ Gemini Engages
♋ Cancer Nurtures
♌ Leo Embraces
♍ Virgo Improves
♎ Libra Commits
♏ Scorpio Manages
♐ Sagittarius Views
♑ Capricorn Climbs
♒ Aquarius Herds
♓ ♇ Pluto Unearths

Planets

☉ Sun Spirit
☽ Moon Emotes
☿ Mercury Thinks
♀ Venus Feels
♂ Mars Acts
♃ Jupiter Expands
♄ Saturn Contracts
♅ Uranus Disrupts
♆ Neptune Envisions
♇ ♇ Pluto Unearths

Aspects

☌ Conjunct 0° Aligns
|| Parallel 0° Equals
⚹ Sextile 60° Helps
□ Square 90° Works
△ Trine 120° Supports
☍ Opposition 180° Counters

AUGUST 2025

Sunday	Monday	Tuesday
☽♐ *♂ **31**		
Tisha B'Av **B** △♄△♅⚹♇△♀ ☽♐ **3** ☉△☽ ☍♓	☽♐ **4**	☽♑ **5** 10:03am □♂□♄□♆□♇ 8:28am - 10:03am
☽♓ **10** △♀△♃ ♂||♆ ☿△♀ □♅ 11:54pm	**F** ☽♓ **11** ♀☌♃ ♄⚹♅ ☿ Dx	Perseid Meteors Peak ☽♈ **12** ♂⚹♅☌♆⚹♇⚹♀ 3:32am ☍♂ 3:32am
☽♊ **17** ☿⚹♂	☽♋ **18** ☉⚹☽ 12:04pm □♄□♆ 4:52am - 12:04pm	☽♋ **19** ♂♃ ☐♂
☽♍ **24** *♃ □□♅	♀ Enters ♌ 9:26am **H** ☽♎ **25** *♀△♅△♀ 7:07am △♄△♆ 6:53am - 7:07am	Ganesh Shaturthi ☽♎ **26** ♂♂*⚹♀ ♀△♅ ♀*♅ □♃ 7:06pm

All calculations are Pacific Clock Time (PST & PDT)

Leo the Lion to Virgo the Virgin

Wednesday	Thursday	Friday	Saturday
		1st Quarter ☽ 5:41am **A** ☾♏ **1** △♃ □☿ ☿□♄ ♀□♄ ♀□♆	☾♐ **2** *♂ 11:00pm 6:06pm - 11:00pm
♂ Enters ♎ 4:23pm **C** ☾♑ **6** ☍♃ 10:39am	**D** △♂△⚹♅*♄♂♇ ☾♒ **7** 6:17pm —— 6:17pm	☾♒ **8** ☌△♅ ♂☍♇	Full ☽ 12:54am 16° ♒ Raksha Bandhan **E** ☾♓ **9** ☉⊟☿ ☉☌♀ ♂☍♆ 11:49pm 12:54am - 11:49pm
Lefthander's Day ☾♈ **13** ☉△☽ □♃□♀ 3:53pm	☾♉ **14** ☿☌♂ ☉∥☽ 6:21am □♇□☿	3rd Quarter ☽ 10:11pm ☾♉ **15** *♃*♀ ♂∥♄ ☉□☽ 10:11pm	Krishna Janmashtami ☾♊ **16** *♄☌♅*♀♆△♀*♇△♂ 9:00am —— 9:00am
♀△♄*♅△♆ ☾♌ **20** 4:16pm ♂☍♇ 5:26am - 4:16pm	*♂♂☌ ☾♌ **21**	☉ Enters ♍ 1:33pm **G** ☾♍ **22** ☉△☽ 10:23pm New ☽ 11:06pm 0° ♍ 1:33pm - 10:23pm	☾♍ **23** ♀∥♅ ☉∥☽ □♅
I ☾♏ **27** 6:26pm □♇ —— 6:26pm	☾♏ **28** ♅*♆ ☉*☽ □♀	☾♏ **29** △♃ □♂ 5:46pm	1st Quarter ☽ 11:24pm ☾♐ **30** △♄△♀*♇△♀ 7:04am ☉□☽ ☍♅ —— 7:04am

Add 1 Hour for Mountain Time (MT) Add 2 Hours for Central Time (CT) Add 3 Hours for Eastern Time (ET)

September Forecast

Lots of Celestial activity among Personal and Outer Planets. BIG EVENTS: Two Eclipses involving, the 7th and 21st. Expect a strong polarity between the personal and public lives. Focus on yourself because outer events are beyond your control, but don't want to feel helpless! A fast Mercury helps tasks move quickly. Venus enters Virgo so focus on personal health. With Saturn, Uranus, Neptune and Pluto Retrograde, outer affairs feel stalled. But Jupiter in Cancer means commercial opportunities will improve for home-based businesses and those focused on the home. Jupiter will turn Retrograde November 11th, expect a slowdown then. Saturn turns Direct late in the month, expect headwinds for conventional businesses. Mars enters Scorpio at the Equinox, a position of feminine power, so be strategic. A good time to address difficult tasks connected to shared resources. Where this is in your chart power is waiting to be used. Scorpio drive very carefully during this Transit until the 4th of December. **A – 1st -** Saturn Retrogrades into Pisces, so expect to feel like you are retracing practical issues that you dealt with before, and a couple of joint pains may resurface. **B – 2nd -** A fast moving Mercury enters Virgo, its feminine Ruling sign. This is the optimal responsive career position for the Winged Messenger. Coupled with a very practical Sun Trine Capricorn Moon, this is a great day to initiate any project that requires dexterity, precision and brings you visibility. **C – 3rd -** That Mercury Square Uranus in Gemini can trigger great ideas, but also arguments about how things should be done. **D – 5th -** Uranus turns Retrograde at 1 degree Gemini, further slowing issues of politics and commerce, but it could also wind down talks of conflict. **E – 7th -** BOOM! The Total Lunar Eclipse at 15 degrees Pisces and Virgo may cause communication and infrastructure problems. Pisces and Virgo, pay attention because this impacts you emotionally and physically. Your intuition gets a jolt so take some longer walks to let your body process that. Everyone needs to pay attention to where this lands in your chart because it is being activated. The two weeks from now until the Solar Eclipse on the 21st may be emotionally difficult for some people so be kind and graceful. **F – 10th –** The Aries Void Of Course Moon in the first half of the day may make the morning erratic. **G – 11th & 12th –** Two White Circle Days in a row. On the 11th this Sun Trine Moon after the Full Moon is a good time to move projects along. On the 12th the Sextiles between the Sun and Mercury to Jupiter can open doors. That lineup of supportive Lunar Aspects will make people anxious to engage. **H – 18th -** Mercury traveled quickly across the thirty degrees of Virgo to get to Libra in eighteen days, so all the communication tasks are easy to move along. Mercury in the Sign of the Scales does encourage some patient weighing of issues, so expect some decisions to take a little longer.

I – 19th - Venus enters Virgo which is a deeply personal position so expect those who are close to you to want to share their concerns about relationships and health. **J – 21st -** The Partial Solar Eclipse at 29 degrees Virgo at the New Moon, will likely be intense because the last degree of a Sign is the epitome of that energy. It opposes Saturn in Pisces and Neptune in Aries so there will be a powerful incentive to focus on your own well-being, because the great affairs of the world will seem to be 'way over there,' out of your control. **K – 22nd -** The Sun enters Libra at the Fall Equinox, leading Mercury and the Moon, and supported by Uranus. This is the same day that Mars enters the powerful Sign of Scorpio. It is a good time to seek partners in order to act because the days and nights are equally long and balanced. *Libra, begin counting down to your Solar Return!* **L – 23rd -** That day long Void Of Course Moon in Libra could be distracting even though the Sun is making supportive Trines to Uranus and Pluto. But it is Opposed to Neptune, so this a potentially chaotic day, so tread lightly.

• •

Mercury☿ 27° Leo♌ enters Virgo♍ on the 2nd at 6:22am, enters Libra♎ on the 18th at 3:05am. Venus♀ 7° Leo♌ enters Virgo♍ on the 19th at 5:38am. Mars♂ 16° Libra♎ enters Scorpio♏ on the 22nd at 12:54am. Jupiter♃ 17° Cancer♋. Saturn♄Rx 0° Aries♈ enters Pisces♓ on the 1st at 1:05am. Uranus♅ 1° Gemini♊ turns Rx on the 5th at 9:51pm at 1° Gemini♊. Neptune♆ Rx 1° Aries♈. Pluto♇ Rx 1° Aquarius♒.

Signs

♈ Aries Begins
♉ Taurus Owns
♊ Gemini Engages
♋ Cancer Nurtures
♌ Leo Embraces
♍ Virgo Improves
♎ Libra Commits
♏ Scorpio Manages
♐ Sagittarius Views
♑ Capricorn Climbs
♒ Aquarius Herds
♓ Pisces Dreams

Planets

☉ Sun Spirit
☽ Moon Emotes
☿ Mercury Thinks
♀ Venus Feels
♂ Mars Acts
♃ Jupiter Expands
♄ Saturn Contracts
♅ Uranus Disrupts
♆ Neptune Envisions
♇ Pluto Unearths

Aspects

☌ Conjunct 0° Aligns
∥ Parallel 0° Equals
✶ Sextile 60° Helps
□ Square 90° Works
△ Trine 120° Supports
☍ Opposition 180° Counters

SEPTEMBER 2025

Sunday	Monday	Tuesday
	♄ Enters ♓ 1:05am **A** △☿ ☾♑ **1** 6:44pm □☿□♆ Labor Day 6:38pm - 6:44pm	♀ Enters ♍ 6:22am **B** ☾♑ **2** ☉△☽
Full ☾ 11:08am 15° ♓ Total ☾ Eclipse **E** △♃ ☾♓ **7** ☉☍☽ ☍☿ Grandparents Day	♂♄♆※✶♇ ☾♈ **8** 11:36am 10:43am - 11:36am	California Admission △♀ ☾♈ **9** ☉∥☽ □♃☍♂ 11:53pm
3rd Quarter ☾ 3:32am ✶♀△♂ ☾♋ **14** ☉□☽ 5:29pm □☿□♄□♆ 3:46pm - 5:29pm	☾♋ **15** ♀☌♂	♂♃✶☿△♇ ☾♌ **16** ☉✶☽ 10:19pm □♂ 8:13pm - 10:19pm
New ☾ 12:53pm 29° ♍ Partial ☉ Eclipse **J** △♅△♇ ☉☌☽ ☾♎ **21** ☉∥☽ 2:40pm ☍♄☍♆ 12:53pm - 2:40pm	☉ Enters ♎ 11:19am Fall Equinox **K** ☾♎ **22** ☉∥☽ ♂ Enters ♏ 12:54am Navratri	Rosh Hashanah ☉☌♀ ☉△♅ **L** ☾♎ **23** ☉∥♄ ☉♂♂ □♃ 9:01am
✶☿ ☾♐ **28** □♄ 10:43pm	1st Quarter ☾ 4:53pm ✶♂ ☾♑ **29** ☉□☽ 2:54am □♆ 2:54am	△♀ ☾♑ **30** ☉∥♄ □☿☍♃

All calculations are Pacific Clock Time (PST & PDT)

Virgo the Virgin to Libra the Scales

Wednesday	Thursday	Friday	Saturday
C ☽♑ **3** ☿□♅ □♂♂♂♃	☽≈ **4** ✶♄✶♆△♅♂♇ 3:31am ♂□♃ 3:07am - 3:31am	The Prophet's Birthday **D** ☽≈ **5** △♂ ♅Rx 1:51pm ♀♇	☽♓ **6** 8:54am □♅ ---- 8:54am
F ☽♉ **10** 1:03pm □♀ ---- 1:03pm	Patriot Day **G** ☽♉ **11** △☿✶♃ ⊙△☽ □♀	☽♊ **12** ✶♄✶♆△♅♂♇ ☿✶♃ 2:38pm ⊙✶♃ 1:13pm - 2:38pm	☽♊ **13** △♂☿
Constitution Day ☽♌ **17** △♆✶♅ ☿♂♄ ♂♇	♀ Enters ♎ 3:05am **H** ☽♌ **18** ☿△♇ △♅ ☿♂♅	♀ Enters ♍ 5:38am **I** ☽♍ **19** ✶♂♂♀ 5:22am □♅ 5:21am - 5:22am	☽♍ **20** ✶♃ ☿∥♆ ♀□♅ ⊙♂♄
☽♏ **24** ♂♂✶♀ ⊙∥♆ 2:00am ♂□♇ □♇ ---- 2:00am	☽♏ **25** △♃	☽♐ **26** △♄△♆△♇ ⊙✶☽ 2:36pm ♂♅ 10:43am - 2:36pm	☽♐ **27** □♀

Add 1 Hour for Mountain Time (MT)   Add 2 Hours for Central Time (CT)   Add 3 Hours for Eastern Time (ET)

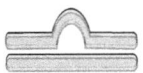

October Forecast

This Month starts unfocused until the New Moon gets it on track. This time of the year days are getting shorter, so determine the best way to manage the resources you've gathered. The sections on the New Moon and the Scorpio Ingress say it all. And there is a bonus piece about the meaning of Halloween! **A – 2nd** - The Libra Sun is Trine the Aquarius Moon, and Square Mars in Scorpio, before the Full Moon. You can accomplish a great deal by finding partners who are good at taking the initiative, while sublimating your own needs into those of the group. **B – 6th** - The Full Moon at 14 degrees Aries and Libra about twelve hours after Mercury enters Scorpio is filled with martial energy so watch your temper, tune out the static, and drive defensively. **C – 7th** - With Jupiter Square the Moon and Mercury Square Pluto, while the Moon is Void Of Course in Aries for the second half of the day, there could be a host of impetuous actions happening, so be careful. **D – 13th** - Venus enters Libra, until the 6th of November so focus on your relationships that you consider a fair cooperation. **E – 14th** - With the Moon in Leo and Venus Trine both Pluto and Uranus, they make three supportive Lunar Aspects so this is a good day to begin projects that include technology, style, law and relationships. **F – 16th** - With the Sun in Libra Square Jupiter in Cancer, issues between what's good for 'us' and what's good for 'me' may come up. With the Moon Void Of Course in Leo until late morning, the day could go off the rails. Once the Moon enters Virgo and Squares Uranus, you should proactively use your technology, otherwise there could be glitches as it begs for attention.

G – 21st – This is an extremely focused New Moon. There will be a sense that the players in the game are clearly identified. That's because Venus in Libra, Mars in Scorpio and Jupiter in Cancer are dignified Signs, two Rulers and one Exalted. They are clearly defined roles that work especially well in the world of career and public life.

With Jupiter loosely Square the New Moon the conflict between businesses focused on personal gain, and what society considers fair will be highlighted. With Mercury Conjunct Mars, loosely Trine both Saturn and Jupiter, you can leverage your ideas very successfully. This is a great time to listen to the ideas of young people and harness that energy.   **H – 22nd** - The Sun enters Scorpio as Neptune backs into Pisces, joining the Moon, Mars and Mercury, so feminine power is strong now, strategize about difficult subjects and make decisions that will help your future. *Scorpio, begin counting down to your Solar Return!* **I – 28th** - A lineup of supportive Lunar Aspects makes this a very productive, social day, so take advantage of that.

J – 29th - Mercury enters Sagittarius, a position that works well in home life due to its optimism and great sense of humor. But Mercury is slowing, to turn Retrograde on November 9th and subsequently back into Scorpio later in the Month. So, use that Mercurial energy now to accomplish communication projects, commercial and interactive tasks, and anything where dexterity is important. The mix of supportive and challenging planetary Aspects could make this a tricky day because we are turning corners and aiming for new goals.

Halloween has a Scorpio Sun and a Pisces Moon so expect creative and spooky costumes. This Celtic holiday celebrated the harvest's end. They it bonfires and wore costumes to dispel bad spirits. The fire destroyed any residual mold and fungus that could damage future crops before spreading the mineral rich ash on the fields. As the nights grew longer, nature spirits and ghosts were more visible. By dressing children in scary costumes, it taught children that they didn't need to be afraid, because they were much scarier than any ghosts.

• •

Mercury☿ 21° Libra♎ enters Scorpio♏ on the 6th at 9:40am, enters Sagittarius♐ on the 29th at 4:01am. Venus♀ 14° Virgo♍ enters Libra♎ on the 13th at 2:18pm. Mars♂ 6° Scorpio♏. Jupiter♃ 22° Cancer♋. Saturn♄Rx 27° Pisces♓. Uranus♅ Rx 1° Gemini♊. Neptune♆ Rx 0° Aries♈ enters Pisces♓ on the 22nd at 2:46am. Pluto♇ Rx 1° Aquarius♒ turns Direct on the 13th at 7:52pm at 1° Aquarius♒.

Signs

- ♈ Aries Begins
- ♉ Taurus Owns
- ♊ Gemini Engages
- ♋ Cancer Nurtures
- ♌ Leo Embraces
- ♍ Virgo Improves
- ♎ Libra Commits
- ♏ Scorpio Manages
- ♐ Sagittarius Views
- ♑ Capricorn Climbs
- ♒ Aquarius Herds
- ♓ Pisces Dreams

Planets

- ☉ Sun Spirit
- ☽ Moon Emotes
- ☿ Mercury Thinks
- ♀ Venus Feels
- ♂ Mars Acts
- ♃ Jupiter Expands
- ♄ Saturn Contracts
- ♅ Uranus Disrupts
- ♆ Neptune Envisions
- ♇ Pluto Unearths

Aspects

- ☌ Conjunct 0° Aligns
- ∥ Parallel 0° Equals
- ✶ Sextile 60° Helps
- □ Square 90° Works
- △ Trine 120° Supports
- ☍ Opposition 180° Counters

OCTOBER 2025

Sunday	Monday	Tuesday
☽♈ **5** 9:47pm △♃☌♄☌♆☌♅ ☉∥☽ ☌♀ 5:29pm - 9:47pm	Full ☽ 8:47pm 14° ♈ **B** ☽♈ **6** ☉☍☽ ♀ enters ♏ 9:40am	Sukkot **C** ☽♉ **7** 10:12pm ♀□♄ □♃ 11:23am - 10:12pm
☽♋ **12** △♃☿ □♆	♀ Enters ♎ 2:18pm 3rd Quarter ☽ 11:12am **D** ☽♋ **13** △♂☌♃△♄ ☿∥♂ ☉□☽ ☌♀ ♀ Dx Indigenous Peoples Day 10:04pm	Shemini Atzeret **E** ☽♌ **14** 3:46am ♀△♃ ♀△♅ ☌♀ - 3:46am ✶♀△♃✶♅
☽♎ **19** ☌♀	Diwali ☽♎ **20** ☿☌♂ □♃	New ☽ 5:24am 28° ♎ **G** ☽♏ **21** 8:41am ☉☌☽ □♀ 5:24am - 8:41am
☽♑ **26** ☉✶☽ 9:41am - 9:52am □♄□♆	☽♑ **27** ♂△♃ □♀	**I** ☽♒ **28** 8:55pm ✶♂✶♄✶♀✶♆△♅☌♀ ✶♃ 8:37pm - 8:55pm

All calculations are Pacific Clock Time (PST & PDT)

Libra the Scales to Scorpio the Scorpion

Wednesday	Thursday	Friday	Saturday
⚹♄⚹♆△♅☌♇ ☾♒ **1** ☿□♃ 12:51pm 8:33am - 12:51pm	Yom Kippur Dussehra **A** ☾♒ **2** ☉△☽ □♂	△☿ ☾♓ **3** 7:06pm □♅ 11:14am - 7:06pm	△♂ ☾♓ **4**
Draconid Meteors Peak ☾♉ **8** ♀⚹♃ □♇☍☿☍♂	⚹♃△♀⚹♄⚹♆☌♅ ☾♊ **9** 10:11pm 5:30pm - 10:11pm	△♇ ☾♊ **10**	☾♋ **11** ☉△☽ ♀☍♄ 11:36pm □♄□♀ 7:55pm - 11:36pm
Simchat Torah ☾♌ **15** ☉⚹☽ □☿□♂ 10:05pm ----------	**F** ☾♍ **16** ☉□♃ 11:05am □♅ ---------- 11:05am	⚹☿⚹♂ ☾♍ **17**	⚹♃△♅△♇ ☾♎ **18** ♀∥♆ 9:01pm ☍♄☍♆ 2:10pm - 9:01pm
☉ Enters ♏ 8:50pm **H** ☾♏ **22** ♆ Enters ♓ 2:46am Orionid Meteors	Orionid Meteors ☌♂☌☿△♃△♄△♆ ☾♐ **23** 9:18pm ☍♅ 9:13pm - 9:18pm	⚹♇ ☾♐ **24** ☿△♃ ♀∥♄ ☉□♇	⚹♀ ☾♐ **25** ☿△♄
☿ Enters ♐ 4:01am 1st Quarter ☽ 9:20am **J** ☾♒ **29** ♂△♄ ☿△♆ ☉□☽ ☿☍♅ 11:15pm ----------	△♀ ☾♒ **30** ☉∥☽ ☿⚹♇ □♂ ----------	Halloween ☾♓ **31** ☿∥♇ ☉△☽ 4:45am □♅□☿ ---------- 4:45am	

Add 1 Hour for Mountain Time (MT) Add 2 Hours for Central Time (CT) Add 3 Hours for Eastern Time (ET)

November Forecast

This month is filled with Changes. The 1st and 3rd weeks are potentially exciting. Jupiter Turns Retrograde and Saturn turns Direct so the Bull Market turns into a Bear, protecting their assets rather than risking them. With the Outer Planets Retrograde, global affairs are stymied. Focus on your personal wellbeing and tune out the noise. *The symbol for Scorpio was Aquila, the Eagle. It was changed when the male early-Christian Priests* rebranded the Zodiac to cast feminine power in a negative light.

A – 4th - Mars enters optimistic Sagittarius and Opposes Uranus. Could be an argumentative day with outbursts. **B – 5th** - The Full Moon may be diffused lacking other Aspects. A good day to respond rather than initiate, but add some levity to your home life.

C – 6th - Venus enters Scorpio, a deeply personal position that works especially well in your family life by encouraging careful management of resources, and confidentiality. **D – 7th** - Uranus, after dipping its toes into Gemini, backs into Taurus, so we may feel like we are revisiting issues related to the climate and economy. **E – 9th** - Mercury turns Retrograde Conjunct the red giant Star Antares so tempers may flare. Mercury backs into Scorpio, turning Direct on the 29th.

F – 11th - Jupiter turns Retrograde and remains retrograde until mid-March of 2026. Expect the economy to still be steady but slow.

G – 12th – Mercury Conjunct Mars triggers some people to feel a anxious and impulsive, especially Fire Signs. **H – 16th** - The Scorpio Sun Trine Jupiter in Cancer will open the doors for opportunity and international connections. **I – 18th** - Mercury Retrogrades into Scorpio so expect some turbulence. **J – 19th** - A chaotic New Moon opposite Uranus Conjunct the Pleiades and supported by Jupiter and Saturn. Emotional scars may resurface, address them from your experience and wisdom. **K – 20th** - Mercury backs across the Sun amid multiple Outer Planet Aspects, this day will sizzle. Don't overload your nervous system.

L – 21st - The Sun enters Sagittarius, joining Mars and the Moon, so it will feel like the page turned and things lightened up. The Fall wind blow the leaves off the trees and vistas expand. The Sun makes Aspects to Uranus and Neptune makaing hidden designs suddenly becoming visible. *Sagittarius, begin counting down to your Solar Return!*

M – 22nd - Coming out of left field, Retrograde Mercury makes Aspects to Jupiter and Saturn so expect surprisingly good economic news that will boost the general optimism. **N – 24th -** With Mercury Conjunct Venus and both of them making supportive Aspects to the Moon, this is a social and productive day, although there may be some work issues that get in the way. **O – 27th - On Thanksgiving Day**, Saturn Turns Direct at 25 degrees Pisces, a position that inclines people to worry about their foundations. With Saturn moving forward and picking up speed, people will be focused on creating the future they believe in. When Saturn enters Aries on February 13, 2026, it will Conjunct Neptune at a point of tremendous leverage. This happens just days before the New Moon in Aquarius, the Lunar New Year which is the seed for the coming growing season. So that message will be tightly woven into the coming year.

P – 29th - Mercury turns Direct at 20 degrees Scorpio, a point known for brilliance. A lineup of supportive Lunar Aspects is spread throughout the day, while Venus Opposes Uranus. Expect an exciting, social, but possibly frustrating time. **Q – 30th -** Venus leaves deeply feminine Scorpio for socially flighty Sagittarius, joining the Sun and Mars, so make a point to get out more and connect with those who inspire hope and fun in your life.

• •

Mercury☿ 2° Sagittarius♐ turns Rx on the 9th at 11:01am at 6° Sagittarius♐, enters Scorpio♏ on the 18th at 7:20pm, turns Direct on the 29th at 9:38am at 20° Scorpio♏. Venus♀ 22° Libra♎ enters Scorpio♏ on the 6th at 2:39pm, enters Sagittarius♐ on the 30th at 2:13pm. Mars♂ 27° Scorpio♏ enters Sagittarius♐ on the 4th at 5:00am. Jupiter♃ 24° Cancer♋ turns Rx on the 11th at 8:41am at 25° Cancer♋. Saturn♄Rx 25° Pisces♓ turns Direct on the 27th at 7:51pm at 25° Pisces♓. Uranus⛢ Rx 0° Gemini♊ enters Taurus♉ on the 7th at 6:21pm. Neptune♆ Rx 29° Pisces♓. Pluto♇ 1° Aquarius♒.

Signs

♈ Aries Begins
♉ Taurus Owns
♊ Gemini Engages
♋ Cancer Nurtures
♌ Leo Embraces
♍ Virgo Improves
♎ Libra Commits
♏ Scorpio Manages
♐ Sagittarius Views
♑ Capricorn Climbs
♒ Aquarius Herds
♓ Pisces Dreams

Planets

☉ Sun Spirit
☽ Moon Emotes
☿ Mercury Thinks
♀ Venus Feels
♂ Mars Acts
♃ Jupiter Expands
♄ Saturn Contracts
♅ Uranus Disrupts
♆ Neptune Envisions
♇ Pluto Unearths

Aspects

☌ Conjunct 0° Aligns
∥ Parallel 0° Equals
✶ Sextile 60° Helps
□ Square 90° Works
△ Trine 120° Supports
☍ Opposition 180° Counters

NOVEMBER 2025

Sunday	Monday	Tuesday
♀ Enters ♐ 12:13pm **Q** ☾♈ 30 ☉△☽ ♀☌♆		
Daylight Time Ends △♃☌♄△☌♂♂♅✶♀△☿ ☾♈ 2 ♀□♃ 7:39am NYC Marathon 7:15am - 7:39am	☾♈ 3 ♂△♅	♂ Enters ♐ 5:00am Election Day **A** ☾♉ 4 ♂♂♅ 8:15am □♃☌♀□♀ 3:21am - 8:15am
E ☾♋ 9 ☉△☽ ♀ Rx	♂♃△♄△♆✶♅△☌△♀ ☾♌ 10 9:33am ☌♂□♀ 9:22am - 9:33am	3rd Quarter ☽ 9:27pm Veterans Day **F** ☾♌ **11** ☿∥♆ ♃ Rx ☉□☽
H ☾♎ 16 ☉△♃	Leonid Meteors Peak ☾♏ 17 ☿✶♀ 1:44pm ☉△♄ □♃☌♀ 3:50am - 1:44pm	☿ Enters ♏ 7:20pm **I** ☾♏ 18 ☉∥☽ ♂♂
☾♑ 23 ☿∥♆ ☉✶♀✶☿✶♄	**N** ✶♀✶☿✶♄ ☾♑ 24 ☿♂♂ ♂♃	△♅✶♆✶♇ ☾♒ 25 ☉∥☽ 2:15am ☉✶♀ 1:09am - 2:15am

All calculations are Pacific Clock Time (PST & PDT)

Scorpio the Scorpion to Sagittarius the Archer

Wednesday	Thursday	Friday	Saturday
			All Saints Day ☾ ♓ **1**
Full ☽ 5:19am 13° ♉ **B** ☾ ♉ **5** ⋯ *✶♃ ☉♂☽ ⸻	♀ Enters ♏ 2:39pm **C** *♄*♆♂♅△♀ ☾ ♊ **6** ⋯ ♂*♇ 7:20am ♂♂♇ 7:10am - 7:20am	♅ Enters ♉ 6:21pm **D** ☾ ♊ **7** ⋯ ♀□♇ □♄	△♀ **☾ ♋ 8** ⋯ 7:05am □♆ 6:31am - 7:05am
Taurid Meteors Peak **G** ☾ ♍ **12** ☿♂♂ 3:51pm □♅ 3:38pm - 3:51pm	*♀ ☾ ♍ **13** ⋯ □☿□♂	*♃ ☿∥♂ ☾ ♍ **14** ☉*☽ ♂♄	△♅△♀*☿*♂ ☾ ♎ **15** ⋯ 1:43am ♂♆ 1:08am - 1:43am
New ☽ 10:47pm 28° ♏ **J**△♃△♄♂☿ ☉♂☽ ☾ ♏ **19** ☉∥♇ △△♀ ♀♂♅	**K** △♀*♃ ♅*♆ ☾ ♐ **20** ☉♂♅ 2:25am ♂♅ 1:24am - 2:25am	☉ Enters ♐ 5:35pm **L** ♂♂ ☾ ♐ **21** ☉△♀ ☉♂♅	**M** ☾ ♑ **22** ♀△♃ 2:52pm □♄□♆ 1:47pm - 2:52pm
*♂ ♀△♀ ☾ ≈ **26** ⋯ ♀△♄ □☿ ♀△♃	1st Quarter ☽ 10:58pm Thanksgiving Day **O** ♄ Dx ☾ ♓ **27** ☿∥♀ 11:23am ☉♂☽ □♀□♅ 9:52am - 11:23am	Black Friday ☾ ♓ **28** ⋯ □♂	Small Business Saturday **P** △♀△♃♂♄△♀*♅♂♆*♇ ☾ ♈ **29** ♀ Dx 5:06pm ♀♂♅ 4:04pm - 5:06pm

Add 1 Hour for Mountain Time (MT) Add 2 Hours for Central Time (CT) Add 3 Hours for Eastern Time (ET)

December Forecast

Optimistic Jupiter holds sway over the first part of the month so emulate those Jovian qualities, be expansive, generous, scholarly, and well traveled. This is a good time to search for gifts from faraway places to share with loved ones. That's why our favorite seasonal scents are spices from tropical islands from the other side of the Earth. Expect the first part of the month to be especially variable, with plenty of movement, getting things done in an intuitive, instinctive way. Once the Sun enters Capricorn it will feel more serious, but with Mercury and Venus still in Sagittarius, a certain lightness will remain.

Remember to get your 2026 Planetary Calendar.

A – 1st - A Day long Void Of Course Moon in Aries could take you off course so make a list of tasks. **B – 4th -** The Moon opposes Venus, just before the Full Moon at 13 degrees Gemini and Sagittarius. The lunation isn't getting much support or structure from the other Planets. So, expect to feel less pressure to get things done, and be more inclined to focus on your relationships until the New Moon on the 19th. This is not a bad strategy to pursue in December! **C – 6th -** A pleasant Mercury Trine Jupiter makes this a good time for serious, heart to heart conversations. **D – 10th -** Neptune turns Direct at 29 degrees Pisces so there will be a sense of the economy nudging forward again. Mercury Opposing Uranus will stimulate outbursts. **E – 11th -** Mercury enters Sagittarius, joining Venus, the Sun and Mars, so with the Moon in Virgo and Saturn and Neptune in Pisces, the Mutable Signs that are concerned with people's needs will be highlighted. Focus on people rather than issues. This is the time of year when charities ramp up fundraising campaigns so expect them to be especially evident this year. Mercury will enter Capricorn just after the New Year. But meantime, Mercury in Sagittarius will make holiday shopping fun, but inclined to excesses, so watch the credit cards.

F – 13th - The Moon Sextile Venus while Mercury Sextiles Pluto is making this another good Saturday for socializing and conversations.

G – 14th - Mars enters Capricorn, a good career position that connects it to Saturn. Mars will be there until late January. If you have the Sun, Rising or Mars in Capricorn you will find your energy levels higher, but watch out for being impulsive.

H – 19th - At the New Moon at 28 degrees Sagittarius, the theme of focusing on people rather than ideas or jobs continues. There will be a very obvious balancing act between those who are optimistic and the worriers. Be prepared for unexpected events, climatic or financial, happening close to the New Moon thanks to an exact Quincunx to Uranus in Taurus. **I – 20th -** The day after the New Moon some powerful Squares may signal a turning point, so manage it carefully, with emotional control. **J – 21st -** At the Winter Solstice, the shortest days of the year, the Sun moves into Capricorn joining Mars. The Sun in Capricorn is a deeply personal position, but the Mars in Capricorn is very social so be prepared to stay true to yourself, while showing up for everyone else. *Capricorn, begin counting down to your Solar Return!* **K – 24th –** Venus enters Capricorn on Christmas Eve and will be there until mid-January. This is a good time to celebrate our ancestors, especially the grandmothers. This position symbolizes the grandmother who passes on the rules and history of the family and takes pride in seeing her children and grandchildren make their way in the world. **L – 25th -** ***Christmas*** has lovely aspects to make this an easy day. The month winds down with a mix of Aspects that are mostly supportive. ***Happy New Year!***

....

Mercury☿ 20° Scorpio♏ enters Sagittarius♐ on the 11th at 2:39pm. Venus♀ 0° Sagittarius♐ enters Capricorn♑ on the 24th at 8:25am. Mars♂ 19° Sagittarius♐ enters Capricorn♑ on the 14th at 11:33pm. Jupiter♃Rx 24° Cancer♋. Saturn♄ 25° Pisces♓. Uranus♅Rx 29° Taurus♉. Neptune♆ Rx 29° Pisces♓ turns Direct on the 10th at 4:22am at 29° Pisces♓. Pluto♇ 1° Aquarius♒.

Signs

♈ Aries Begins
♉ Taurus Owns
♊ Gemini Engages
♋ Cancer Nurtures
♌ Leo Embraces
♍ Virgo Improves
♎ Libra Commits
♏ Scorpio Manages
♐ Sagittarius Views
♑ Capricorn Climbs
♒ Aquarius Herds
♓ Pisces Dreams

Planets

☉ Sun Spirit
☽ Moon Emotes
☿ Mercury Thinks
♀ Venus Feels
♂ Mars Acts
♃ Jupiter Expands
♄ Saturn Contracts
♅ Uranus Disrupts
♆ Neptune Envisions
♇ ⚴ Pluto Unearths

Aspects

☌ Conjunct 0° Aligns
∥ Parallel 0° Equals
✶ Sextile 60° Helps
□ Square 90° Works
△ Trine 120° Supports
☍ Opposition 180° Counters

DECEMBER 2025

Sunday	Monday	Tuesday
	Cyber Monday **A** ☾ ♉ 1 △♂ 7:12pm □♃□♇ 10:14am - 7:12pm	☾ ♉ 2 ♀✶♇
♂△♃△♄△♀✶♅△♆ ☾ ♌ 7 ♀△♄ 6:47pm ☌♇ 5:44pm - 6:47pm	△♀ ☾ ♌ 8 ♂□♄	△♂ ☾ ♍ 9 ☉△☽ 11:19pm □♀☍♅ 8:56pm - 11:19pm
♂ Enters ♑ 11:33pm *Geminid Meteors* **G** ☾ ♏ 14 ☉✶☽ 7:50pm ♂☌♆ □♃ 7:35pm - 7:50pm	Chanukah First Day ☾ ♏ 15 ☉∥♇ □♀	△♃△♄ ☾ ♏ 16 ☉∥☽ ☉□♄
☉ Enters ♑ 7:02am Winter Solstice **J** ☾ ♐ 21 ✶♀ ☍♃	Ursid Meteors Chanukah (Last Day) △♅✶♆☌♀ ☾ ♒ 22 ☉∥☽ 7:51am 7:40am - 7:51am	✶☿ ☾ ♒ 23 ♀□♆
△♀ ☾ ♈ 28 ☉∥♇ □♃ 6:12pm	△♀△♂ ☉△☽ ☾ ♉ 29 ☿♀ 3:57am ☿△♄ □♇ ---------- 3:57am	✶♃✶♄ ☾ ♉ 30 ♀∥♂

All calculations are Pacific Clock Time (PST & PDT)

Sagittarius the Archer to Capricorn the Sea Goat

Wednesday	Thursday	Friday	Saturday
✶♃✶♄☌⚸✶♆△♇ ☾♊ **3** 6:47pm ♂☍☿ 5:50pm - 6:47pm	Full ☽ 13° ♊ 3:13pm **B** ☾♊ **4** ☉☍☽ ♂☍☿	☾♋ **5** 5:53pm ♂☍☌☍♄☍♆ 4:54pm - 5:53pm	St. Nicholas Day **C** ☾♋ **6** ☿△♃
D ☾♍ **10** ♆Dx ☿☌⚸ ☐♀	♀ Enters ♐ 2:39pm 3rd Quarter ☽ 12:51pm **E** ✶♃ ☾♍ **11** ☿△♆ ☉☐☽ ♂☍♄	△⚸✶♇△♀ ☾♎ **12** 8:03am ☐♂☍♆ 6:50am - 8:03am	"Geminid Meteors" **F** ✶♀ ☾♎ **13** ☿✶♃
△♆✶♇ ☾♐ **17** 8:38am ♂☍♆ 7:23am - 8:38am	☾♐ **18** ♂☌☿	New ☽ 5:43pm 28° ♐ **H** ♂☌ ☾♑ **19** ♀☍♇ ☉☌☽ 8:52pm ☐♄☐♆ 7:40pm - 8:52pm	**I** ♂☌ ☾♑ **20** ☉∥☿ ☉∥♇ ♀☐☿
♀ Enters ♑ 8:25am Christmas Eve **K** ✶♀ ☾♓ **24** 5:08pm ☐⚸ 1:41pm - 5:08pm	Christmas Day **L** ✶♂ ☾♓ **25** ☉✶☽	Kwanzaa (1st Day) △♃☌♄✶⚸☌♀ ☾♓ **26** ☐⚸ 11:03pm —————	1st Quarter ☽ 11:09am ✶♀ ☉∥☿ ☾♈ **27** ☉∥♇ 12:01am ☉☐☽ ☐♀☌♂ ————— 12:01am
New Year's Eve ♂⚸✶♆△♇ ☾♊ **31** 5:12am 4:24am - 5:12am			

Add 1 Hour for Mountain Time (MT)   Add 2 Hours for Central Time (CT)   Add 3 Hours for Eastern Time (ET)

JANUARY 2025

00:00 UT

Day	Sid.t	☉	☽	☿	♀	♂	♃	♄	♅	♆	♇	☊	☊	⚸	⚷	Day
W 1	6 43 36	10♑48'49	23♑55	19♐52	27♒43	1°R55	13°R13	14♓31	23°R38	27♓18	1♒ 4	0°R53	1♈30	20♎34	19♈ 0	W 1
T 2	6 47 32	11°50'00	7♒27	21°10	28°47	1♌35	13♊ 7	14°36	23♉37	27°19	1° 6	0♈42	1°27	20°40	19° 0	T 2
F 3	6 51 29	12°51'10	21°10	22°29	29°51	1°15	13° 0	14°41	23°35	27°20	1° 8	0°34	1°23	20°47	19° 1	F 3
S 4	6 55 26	13°52'21	5♓ 0	23°50	0♓55	0°54	12°54	14°45	23°34	27°20	1° 9	0°29	1°20	20°54	19° 1	S 4
S 5	6 59 22	14°53'31	18°55	25°12	1°58	0°32	12°49	14°50	23°33	27°21	1°11	0°26	1°17	21° 0	19° 1	S 5
M 6	7 3 19	15°54'40	2♈55	26°35	3° 1	0°10	12°43	14°55	23°31	27°22	1°13	0°D26	1°14	21° 7	19° 1	M 6
T 7	7 7 15	16°55'50	16°58	27°58	4° 4	29♋48	12°37	15° 0	23°30	27°23	1°15	0°R26	1°11	21°14	19° 2	T 7
W 8	7 11 12	17°56'58	1♉ 4	29°23	5° 6	29°25	12°32	15° 5	23°29	27°24	1°17	0°26	1° 8	21°20	19° 2	W 8
T 9	7 15 8	18°58'07	15°12	0♑48	6° 8	29° 2	12°27	15°10	23°28	27°26	1°19	0°23	1° 4	21°27	19° 3	T 9
F 10	7 19 5	19°59'15	29°21	2°14	7° 9	28°38	12°22	15°15	23°27	27°27	1°21	0°18	1° 1	21°34	19° 4	F 10
S 11	7 23 1	21° 0'22	13♊27	3°41	8°10	28°15	12°17	15°21	23°26	27°28	1°23	0°10	0°58	21°40	19° 4	S 11
S 12	7 26 58	22° 1'29	27°27	5° 8	9°11	27°51	12°12	15°26	23°25	27°29	1°25	29♓59	0°55	21°47	19° 5	S 12
M13	7 30 55	23° 2'36	11♋17	6°37	10°11	27°27	12° 7	15°31	23°24	27°30	1°27	29°48	0°52	21°54	19° 6	M13
T 14	7 34 51	24° 3'42	24°52	8° 5	11°11	27° 3	12° 3	15°37	23°23	27°31	1°28	29°36	0°49	22° 0	19° 6	T 14
W15	7 38 48	25° 4'48	8♌10	9°35	12°10	26°39	11°59	15°42	23°22	27°33	1°30	29°26	0°45	22° 7	19° 7	W15
T 16	7 42 44	26° 5'53	21° 8	11° 5	13° 9	26°15	11°55	15°48	23°21	27°34	1°32	29°18	0°42	22°14	19° 8	T 16
F 17	7 46 41	27° 6'58	3♍47	12°35	14° 7	25°51	11°51	15°54	23°21	27°35	1°34	29°12	0°39	22°20	19° 9	F 17
S 18	7 50 37	28° 8'02	16° 8	14° 6	15° 5	25°27	11°48	15°59	23°20	27°37	1°36	29° 9	0°36	22°27	19°10	S 18
S 19	7 54 34	29° 9'07	28°14	15°38	16° 2	25° 4	11°44	16° 5	23°19	27°38	1°38	29°D 8	0°33	22°34	19°11	S 19
M20	7 58 31	0♒10'10	10♎ 9	17°10	16°59	24°40	11°41	16°11	23°19	27°39	1°40	29° 8	0°29	22°40	19°12	M20
T 21	8 2 27	1°11'14	21°58	18°43	17°55	24°17	11°38	16°17	23°18	27°41	1°42	29° 9	0°26	22°47	19°14	T 21
W22	8 6 24	2°12'17	3♏47	20°16	18°50	23°54	11°35	16°23	23°18	27°42	1°44	29°R 9	0°23	22°54	19°15	W22
T 23	8 10 20	3°13'19	15°40	21°50	19°45	23°31	11°32	16°29	23°17	27°44	1°46	29° 8	0°20	23° 0	19°16	T 23
F 24	8 14 17	4°14'22	27°43	23°24	20°39	23° 9	11°30	16°35	23°17	27°45	1°48	29° 5	0°17	23° 7	19°18	F 24
S 25	8 18 13	5°15'23	10♐ 2	24°59	21°33	22°47	11°28	16°41	23°17	27°47	1°50	29° 0	0°14	23°13	19°19	S 25
S 26	8 22 10	6°16'25	22°38	26°35	22°26	22°25	11°26	16°47	23°16	27°48	1°52	28°53	0°10	23°20	19°20	S 26
M27	8 26 6	7°17'25	5♑36	28°11	23°18	22° 4	11°24	16°53	23°16	27°50	1°54	28°44	0° 7	23°27	19°22	M27
T 28	8 30 3	8°18'25	18°55	29°48	24° 9	21°44	11°22	17° 0	23°16	27°51	1°56	28°35	0° 4	23°33	19°23	T 28
W29	8 34 0	9°19'24	2♒34	1♒26	25° 0	21°24	11°21	17° 6	23°16	27°53	1°57	28°26	0° 1	23°40	19°25	W29
T 30	8 37 56	10°20'22	16°31	3° 4	25°50	21° 5	11°20	17°12	23°16	27°55	1°59	28°18	29♓58	23°47	19°27	T 30
F 31	8 41 53	11♒21'19	0♓40	4♒43	26♓39	20♋46	11♊19	17♓19	23°D16	27♓56	2♒ 1	28♓13	29♓55	23♎53	19♈28	F 31

FEBRUARY 2025

00:00 UT

Day	Sid.t	☉	☽	☿	♀	♂	♃	♄	♅	♆	♇	♊	☊	⚷	δ	Day
S 1	8 45 49	12♒22 15	14♓58	6♒23	27♓47	20♈28	11♊R18	17♓25	23♉16	27♓58	2♒ 3	28♈R10	29♓51	24♎ 0	19♈30	S 1
S 2	8 49 46	13°23 10	29♓18	8° 3	28°14	20♒10	11 II 17	17°32	23°16	28° 0	2° 5	28°FD 9	29°48	24° 7	19°32	S 2
M 3	8 53 42	14°24 03	13♈38	9°44	29° 0	19°54	11°17	17°39	23°16	28° 2	2° 7	28♈10	29°45	24°13	19°34	M 3
T 4	8 57 39	15°24 55	27°54	11°26	29°45	19°38	11°17	17°45	23°16	28° 3	2° 9	28°11	29°42	24°20	19°36	T 4
W 5	9 1 35	16°25 45	12♉ 3	13° 8	0♈29	19°22	11°17	17°52	23°16	28°R12	2°11	28°R12	29°39	24°27	19°38	W 5
T 6	9 5 32	17°26 35	26° 5	14°52	1°13	19° 8	11°17	17°58	23°17	28° 7	2°13	28°10	29°35	24°33	19°40	T 6
F 7	9 9 29	18°27 22	9 II 59	16°36	1°55	18°54	11°18	18° 5	23°17	28° 9	2°15	28°10	29°32	24°40	19°42	F 7
S 8	9 13 25	19°28 09	23°43	18°20	2°35	18°41	11°18	18°12	23°18	28°11	2°16	28° 6	29°29	24°47	19°44	S 8
S 9	9 17 22	20°28 53	7♋17	20° 6	3°15	18°29	11°19	18°19	23°18	28°13	2°18	28° 1	29°26	24°53	19°46	S 9
M10	9 21 18	21°29 36	20°39	21°52	3°53	18°18	11°20	18°26	23°19	28°14	2°20	27°55	29°23	25° 0	19°48	M10
T11	9 25 15	22°30 18	3♌49	23°39	4°30	18° 7	11°21	18°33	23°19	28°16	2°22	27°48	29°20	25° 7	19°50	T11
W12	9 29 11	23°30 58	16°44	25°27	5° 6	17°57	11°22	18°40	23°20	28°18	2°24	27°43	29°16	25°13	19°52	W12
T13	9 33 8	24°31 37	29°25	27°16	5°40	17°48	11°24	18°46	23°20	28°20	2°26	27°38	29°13	25°20	19°55	T13
F14	9 37 4	25°32 14	11♍52	29° 5	6°13	17°40	11°26	18°53	23°21	28°22	2°27	27°35	29°10	25°27	19°57	F14
S15	9 41 1	26°32 50	24° 5	0♓54	6°44	17°33	11°28	19° 0	23°22	28°24	2°29	27°FD34	29° 7	25°33	19°59	S15
S16	9 44 58	27°33 25	6♎ 7	2°45	7°14	17°26	11°30	19° 8	23°23	28°26	2°31	27°34	29° 1	25°40	20° 2	S16
M17	9 48 54	28°33 58	18° 1	4°36	7°42	17°20	11°33	19°15	23°24	28°28	2°33	27°36	29° 1	25°47	20° 4	M17
T18	9 52 51	29°34 30	29°51	6°27	8° 8	17°15	11°35	19°22	23°25	28°30	2°35	27°38	28°57	25°53	20° 7	T18
W19	9 56 47	0♓35 01	11♏40	8°18	8°33	17°11	11°38	19°29	23°26	28°32	2°36	27°39	28°54	26° 0	20° 9	W19
T20	10 0 44	1°35 31	23°33	10°10	8°56	17° 7	11°41	19°36	23°27	28°34	2°38	27°41	28°51	26° 7	20°12	T20
F21	10 4 40	2°35 59	5♐35	12° 1	9°17	17° 4	11°44	19°43	23°28	28°36	2°40	27°R41	28°48	26°13	20°15	F21
S22	10 8 37	3°36 26	17°52	13°53	9°36	17° 3	11°48	19°50	23°29	28°39	2°42	27°40	28°45	26°20	20°17	S22
S23	10 12 33	4°36 52	0♑37	15°43	9°53	17°D 2	11°51	19°58	23°30	28°41	2°43	27°38	28°41	26°27	20°20	S23
M24	10 16 30	5°37 16	13°25	17°33	10° 7	17° 1	11°55	20° 5	23°31	28°43	2°45	27°35	28°38	26°33	20°23	M24
T25	10 20 27	6°37 39	26°47	19°22	10°20	17° 1	11°59	20°12	23°33	28°45	2°47	27°32	28°35	26°40	20°25	T25
W26	10 24 23	7°38 00	10♒34	21° 9	10°31	17° 2	12° 3	20°19	23°34	28°47	2°48	27°29	28°32	26°47	20°28	W26
T27	10 28 20	8°38 20	24°44	22°54	10°39	17° 4	12° 7	20°27	23°35	28°49	2°50	27°26	28°29	26°53	20°31	T27
F28	10 32 16	9°38 38	9♓13	24°37	10°45	17° 7	12 II 12	20°34	23°37	28°51	2°52	27°25	28°26	27°0	20°34	F28

MARCH 2025 00:00 UT

Day	Sid.t	☉	☽	☿	♀	♂	♃	♄	♅	♆	♇	☊	☊	⚸	⚷	Day
S 1	10 36 13	10♓38'54	23♓55	26♓17	10♈49	17♋10	12♊16	20♓41	23♉38	28♓54	2♒53	27°D24	28♓22	27♎ 7	20♈37	S 1
S 2	10 40 9	11°39'08	8♈43	27°54	10°R50	17°14	12°21	20°49	23°40	28°56	2°55	27♓24	28°19	27°13	20°40	S 2
M 3	10 44 6	12°39'21	23°30	29°26	10°49	17°18	12°26	20°56	23°41	28°58	2°56	27°25	28°16	27°20	20°43	M 3
T 4	10 48 2	13°39'31	8♉ 9	0♈54	10°45	17°24	12°31	21° 3	23°43	29° 0	2°58	27°26	28°13	27°27	20°45	T 4
W 5	10 51 59	14°39'39	22°35	2°17	10°39	17°29	12°37	21°11	23°45	29° 2	2°59	27°27	28°10	27°33	20°48	W 5
T 6	10 55 56	15°39'46	6♊46	3°34	10°31	17°36	12°42	21°18	23°46	29° 5	3° 1	27°28	28° 7	27°40	20°52	T 6
F 7	10 59 52	16°39'50	20°39	4°45	10°19	17°43	12°48	21°26	23°48	29° 7	3° 3	27°R28	28° 3	27°47	20°55	F 7
S 8	11 3 49	17°39'52	4♋13	5°49	10° 6	17°51	12°54	21°33	23°50	29° 9	3° 4	27°28	28° 0	27°53	20°58	S 8
S 9	11 7 45	18°39'52	17°31	6°46	9°49	18° 0	13° 0	21°40	23°52	29°11	3° 5	27°27	27°57	28° 0	21° 1	S 9
M10	11 11 42	19°39'50	0♌33	7°35	9°31	18° 9	13° 6	21°48	23°54	29°14	3° 7	27°26	27°54	28° 7	21° 4	M10
T 11	11 15 38	20°39'45	13°20	8°16	9°10	18°18	13°12	21°55	23°56	29°16	3° 8	27°25	27°51	28°13	21° 7	T 11
W12	11 19 35	21°39'39	25°54	8°49	8°46	18°29	13°19	22° 3	23°58	29°18	3°10	27°24	27°47	28°20	21°10	W12
T 13	11 23 31	22°39'30	8♍16	9°13	8°21	18°39	13°26	22°10	24° 0	29°20	3°11	27°24	27°44	28°27	21°13	T 13
F 14	11 27 28	23°39'19	20°28	9°28	7°53	18°51	13°32	22°17	24° 2	29°23	3°13	27°23	27°41	28°33	21°17	F 14
S 15	11 31 25	24°39'06	2♎31	9°R35	7°24	19° 2	13°39	22°25	24° 4	29°25	3°14	27°D23	27°38	28°40	21°20	S 15
S 16	11 35 21	25°38'52	14°27	9°33	6°52	19°15	13°46	22°32	24° 6	29°27	3°15	27°23	27°35	28°47	21°23	S 16
M17	11 39 18	26°38'35	26°18	9°23	6°20	19°28	13°54	22°40	24° 8	29°29	3°16	27°23	27°32	28°53	21°27	M17
T 18	11 43 14	27°38'17	8♏ 7	9° 5	5°45	19°41	14° 1	22°47	24°10	29°32	3°18	27°R23	27°28	29° 0	21°30	T 18
W19	11 47 11	28°37'57	19°57	8°39	5°10	19°55	14° 9	22°54	24°13	29°34	3°19	27°23	27°25	29° 7	21°33	W19
T 20	11 51 7	29°37'35	1♐51	8° 7	4°33	20° 9	14°16	23° 2	24°15	29°36	3°20	27°23	27°22	29°13	21°37	T 20
F 21	11 55 4	0♈37'11	13°53	7°29	3°56	20°24	14°24	23° 9	24°17	29°38	3°21	27°23	27°19	29°20	21°40	F 21
S 22	11 59 0	1°36'46	26° 8	6°46	3°19	20°40	14°32	23°16	24°20	29°41	3°23	27°D23	27°16	29°27	21°43	S 22
S 23	12 2 57	2°36'19	8♑39	5°58	2°41	20°55	14°40	23°24	24°22	29°43	3°24	27°23	27°12	29°33	21°47	S 23
M24	12 6 53	3°35'50	21°32	5° 8	2° 3	21°12	14°48	23°31	24°24	29°45	3°25	27°23	27° 9	29°40	21°50	M24
T 25	12 10 50	4°35'20	4♒48	4°16	1°26	21°28	14°57	23°39	24°27	29°48	3°26	27°24	27° 6	29°47	21°54	T 25
W26	12 14 47	5°34'47	18°31	3°23	0°49	21°45	15° 5	23°46	24°29	29°50	3°27	27°24	27° 3	29°53	21°57	W26
T 27	12 18 43	6°34'13	2♓40	2°30	0°13	22° 3	15°14	23°53	24°32	29°52	3°28	27°25	27° 0	29°59	22° 0	T 27
F 28	12 22 40	7°33'37	17°14	1°39	29♓38	22°21	15°22	24° 0	24°35	29°54	3°29	27°26	26°57	0♏ 7	22° 4	F 28
S 29	12 26 36	8°32'59	2♈ 7	0°50	29° 4	22°39	15°31	24° 8	24°37	29°57	3°30	27°R26	26°53	0°13	22° 7	S 29
S 30	12 30 33	9°32'19	17°13	0° 4	28°32	22°58	15°40	24°15	24°40	29°59	3°31	27°25	26°50	0°20	22°11	S 30
M31	12 34 29	10♈31'37	2♉21	29♓22	28♓ 1	23♋17	15♊49	24♓22	24♉43	0♈ 1	3♒32	27♓24	26♓47	0♏27	22♈14	M31

APRIL 2025 — 00:00 UT

Day	Sid.t	☉	☽	☿	♀	♂	♃	♄	♅	♆	♇	☊	☊	⚸	⚷	Day
T 1	12 38 26	11♈30'53	17♉23	28°R45	27°R32	23♋36	15♊59	24♓29	24♉45	0♈ 3	3♒33	27°R22	26♓44	0♏33	22♈18	T 1
W 2	12 42 22	12°30'06	2♊11	28♓12	27♓ 5	23°56	16° 8	24°37	24°48	0° 6	3°34	27♓21	26°41	0°40	22°22	W 2
T 3	12 46 19	13°29'18	16°38	27°45	26°40	24°16	16°17	24°44	24°51	0° 8	3°35	27°19	26°38	0°47	22°25	T 3
F 4	12 50 16	14°28'27	0♋40	27°23	26°17	24°36	16°27	24°51	24°54	0°10	3°36	27°18	26°34	0°53	22°29	F 4
S 5	12 54 12	15°27'33	14°18	27° 6	25°56	24°57	16°37	24°58	24°57	0°12	3°37	27°D17	26°31	1° 0	22°32	S 5
S 6	12 58 9	16°26'38	27°31	26°55	25°38	25°19	16°47	25° 5	25° 0	0°14	3°38	27°18	26°28	1° 7	22°36	S 6
M 7	13 2 5	17°25'40	10♌24	26°D50	25°22	25°40	16°56	25°12	25° 2	0°17	3°38	27°19	26°25	1°13	22°39	M 7
T 8	13 6 2	18°24'40	22°57	26°50	25° 8	26° 2	17° 7	25°19	25° 5	0°19	3°39	27°20	26°22	1°20	22°43	T 8
W 9	13 9 58	19°23'37	5♍17	26°56	24°57	26°24	17°17	25°26	25° 8	0°21	3°40	27°22	26°18	1°27	22°46	W 9
T 10	13 13 55	20°22'32	17°25	27° 7	24°49	26°46	17°27	25°33	25°11	0°23	3°41	27°23	26°15	1°33	22°50	T 10
F 11	13 17 51	21°21'25	29°24	27°22	24°43	27° 9	17°37	25°40	25°14	0°25	3°41	27°R23	26°12	1°40	22°54	F 11
S 12	13 21 48	22°20'16	11♎18	27°43	24°39	27°32	17°48	25°47	25°17	0°28	3°42	27°22	26° 9	1°47	22°57	S 12
S 13	13 25 45	23°19'05	23° 9	28° 8	24°D37	27°55	17°58	25°54	25°20	0°30	3°42	27°20	26° 6	1°53	23° 1	S 13
M14	13 29 41	24°17'52	4♏59	28°38	24°39	28°19	18° 9	26° 1	25°24	0°32	3°43	27°17	26° 3	2° 0	23° 4	M14
T 15	13 33 38	25°16'37	16°49	29°11	24°42	28°43	18°19	26° 8	25°27	0°34	3°44	27°12	25°59	2° 7	23° 8	T 15
W16	13 37 34	26°15'20	28°42	29°49	24°48	29° 7	18°30	26°14	25°30	0°36	3°44	27° 7	25°56	2°13	23°11	W16
T 17	13 41 31	27°14'02	10♐40	0♈31	24°56	29°31	18°41	26°21	25°33	0°38	3°45	27° 2	25°53	2°20	23°15	T 17
F 18	13 45 27	28°12'41	22°46	1°16	25° 6	29°56	18°52	26°28	25°36	0°40	3°45	26°57	25°50	2°27	23°19	F 18
S 19	13 49 24	29°11'19	5♑ 2	2° 5	25°18	0♌20	19° 3	26°34	25°39	0°42	3°46	26°54	25°47	2°33	23°22	S 19
S 20	13 53 20	0♉ 9'56	17°33	2°57	25°33	0°45	19°14	26°41	25°43	0°44	3°46	26°51	25°44	2°40	23°26	S 20
M21	13 57 17	1° 8'30	0♒21	3°52	25°49	1°11	19°26	26°48	25°46	0°46	3°46	26°D51	25°40	2°47	23°29	M21
T 22	14 1 14	2° 7'03	13°30	4°50	26° 7	1°36	19°37	26°54	25°49	0°48	3°47	26°51	25°37	2°53	23°33	T 22
W23	14 5 10	3° 5'35	27° 3	5°51	26°28	2° 2	19°48	27° 1	25°52	0°50	3°47	26°52	25°34	3° 0	23°36	W23
T 24	14 9 7	4° 4'04	11♓ 3	6°55	26°50	2°28	20° 0	27° 7	25°56	0°52	3°48	26°54	25°31	3° 7	23°40	T 24
F 25	14 13 3	5° 2'32	25°28	8° 1	27°13	2°54	20°11	27°14	25°59	0°54	3°48	26°R55	25°28	3°13	23°43	F 25
S 26	14 17 0	6° 0'59	10♈17	9°10	27°39	3°20	20°23	27°20	26° 2	0°56	3°48	26°54	25°24	3°20	23°47	S 26
S 27	14 20 56	6°59'23	25°23	10°22	28° 6	3°47	20°35	27°26	26° 6	0°58	3°48	26°52	25°21	3°27	23°50	S 27
M28	14 24 53	7°57'47	10♉38	11°36	28°35	4°14	20°46	27°32	26° 9	1° 0	3°48	26°47	25°18	3°33	23°54	M28
T 29	14 28 49	8°56'08	25°51	12°52	29° 5	4°41	20°58	27°39	26°12	1° 2	3°49	26°41	25°15	3°40	23°57	T 29
W30	14 32 46	9♉54'27	10♊53	14♈10	29♓36	5♌ 8	21♊10	27♓45	26♉16	1♈ 4	3♒49	26♓35	25♓12	3♏47	24♈ 1	W30

MAY 2025

00:00 UT

Day	Sid.t	☉	☽	☿	♀	♂	♃	♄	♅	♆	♇	☊	☊	⚸	⚷	Day
T 1	14 36 43	10♉52'45	25♊34	15♈31	0♈ 9	5♌36	21♊22	27♓51	26♉19	1♈ 6	3♒49	26°R29	25♓ 9	3♏53	24♈ 4	T 1
F 2	14 40 39	11°51'00	9♋49	16°54	0°44	6° 3	21°34	27°57	26°22	1° 8	3°49	26♓23	25° 5	4° 0	24° 8	F 2
S 3	14 44 36	12°49'14	23°35	18°18	1°19	6°31	21°46	28° 3	26°26	1° 9	3°49	26°20	25° 2	4° 7	24°11	S 3
S 4	14 48 32	13°47'25	6♌52	19°45	1°56	6°59	21°59	28° 9	26°29	1°11	3°49	26°18	24°59	4°13	24°15	S 4
M 5	14 52 29	14°45'35	19°44	21°14	2°34	7°27	22°11	28°15	26°33	1°13	3°R49	26°D18	24°56	4°20	24°18	M 5
T 6	14 56 25	15°43'42	2♍14	22°45	3°13	7°55	22°23	28°21	26°36	1°15	3°49	26°19	24°53	4°27	24°21	T 6
W 7	15 0 22	16°41'48	14°27	24°18	3°53	8°24	22°35	28°26	26°40	1°16	3°49	26°20	24°50	4°33	24°25	W 7
T 8	15 4 18	17°39'51	26°28	25°53	4°34	8°53	22°48	28°32	26°43	1°18	3°49	26°R21	24°46	4°40	24°28	T 8
F 9	15 8 15	18°37'53	8♎21	27°30	5°17	9°21	23° 0	28°38	26°47	1°20	3°49	26°20	24°43	4°47	24°31	F 9
S 10	15 12 12	19°35'53	20°11	29° 9	6° 0	9°50	23°13	28°43	26°50	1°22	3°49	26°17	24°40	4°53	24°35	S 10
S 11	15 16 8	20°33'51	1♏59	0♉50	6°44	10°20	23°26	28°49	26°53	1°23	3°49	26°12	24°37	5° 0	24°38	S 11
M12	15 20 5	21°31'47	13°49	2°32	7°29	10°49	23°38	28°54	26°57	1°25	3°48	26° 4	24°34	5° 7	24°41	M12
T 13	15 24 1	22°29'42	25°43	4°17	8°15	11°18	23°51	29° 0	27° 0	1°26	3°48	25°55	24°30	5°13	24°45	T 13
W14	15 27 58	23°27'36	7♐43	6° 4	9° 2	11°48	24° 4	29° 5	27° 4	1°28	3°48	25°44	24°27	5°20	24°48	W14
T 15	15 31 54	24°25'28	19°50	7°53	9°49	12°18	24°16	29°10	27° 7	1°30	3°48	25°33	24°24	5°27	24°51	T 15
F 16	15 35 51	25°23'19	2♑ 4	9°44	10°38	12°48	24°29	29°16	27°11	1°31	3°47	25°23	24°21	5°34	24°54	F 16
S 17	15 39 47	26°21'09	14°29	11°37	11°27	13°18	24°42	29°21	27°14	1°33	3°47	25°15	24°18	5°40	24°57	S 17
S 18	15 43 44	27°18'57	27° 5	13°31	12°17	13°48	24°55	29°26	27°18	1°34	3°47	25° 8	24°15	5°47	25° 1	S 18
M19	15 47 41	28°16'44	9♒56	15°28	13° 7	14°18	25° 8	29°31	27°21	1°36	3°46	25° 5	24°11	5°54	25° 4	M19
T 20	15 51 37	29°14'30	23° 3	17°27	13°58	14°48	25°21	29°36	27°25	1°37	3°46	25° 3	24° 8	6° 0	25° 7	T 20
W21	15 55 34	0♊12'15	6♓30	19°27	14°50	15°19	25°34	29°41	27°28	1°38	3°45	25°D 3	24° 5	6° 7	25°10	W21
T 22	15 59 30	1° 9'58	20°19	21°29	15°43	15°50	25°47	29°45	27°32	1°40	3°45	25°R 3	24° 2	6°14	25°13	T 22
F 23	16 3 27	2° 7'41	4♈31	23°33	16°36	16°20	26° 0	29°50	27°35	1°41	3°44	25° 3	23°59	6°20	25°16	F 23
S 24	16 7 23	3° 5'23	19° 6	25°39	17°29	16°51	26°13	29°55	27°39	1°42	3°44	25° 1	23°56	6°27	25°19	S 24
S 25	16 11 20	4° 3'03	3♉58	27°46	18°23	17°23	26°27	29°59	27°42	1°44	3°43	24°57	23°52	6°34	25°22	S 25
M26	16 15 16	5° 0'43	19° 3	29°55	19°18	17°54	26°40	0♈ 4	27°46	1°45	3°43	24°50	23°49	6°40	25°25	M26
T 27	16 19 13	5°58'22	4♊11	2♊ 4	20°13	18°25	26°53	0° 8	27°49	1°46	3°42	24°41	23°46	6°47	25°28	T 27
W28	16 23 10	6°55'59	19°12	4°15	21° 9	18°57	27° 6	0°13	27°53	1°47	3°42	24°30	23°43	6°54	25°31	W28
T 29	16 27 6	7°53'36	3♋56	6°26	22° 5	19°28	27°20	0°17	27°56	1°49	3°41	24°20	23°40	7° 0	25°34	T 29
F 30	16 31 3	8°51'11	18°16	8°38	23° 1	20° 0	27°33	0°21	28° 0	1°50	3°40	24°11	23°36	7° 7	25°36	F 30
S 31	16 34 59	9♊48'44	2♌ 7	10♊50	23♈58	20♌32	27♊47	0♈25	28♉ 3	1♈51	3♒40	24♓ 4	23♓33	7♏14	25♈39	S 31

JUNE 2025 — 00:00 UT

Day	Sid.t	☉	☽	☿	♀	♂	♃	♄	♅	♆	♇	☊	☊	⚸	⚷	Day
S 1	16 38 56	10♊46'17	15♌30	13♊ 2	24♈56	21♌ 3	28♊ 0	0♈29	28♉ 7	1♈52	3°R39	23°R59	23♓30	7♏20	25♈42	S 1
M 2	16 42 52	11°43'47	28°25	15°14	25°53	21°36	28°13	0°33	28°10	1°53	3♒38	23♓57	23°27	7°27	25°45	M 2
T 3	16 46 49	12°41'17	10♍57	17°25	26°52	22° 8	28°27	0°37	28°13	1°54	3°38	23°D57	23°24	7°34	25°47	T 3
W 4	16 50 46	13°38'45	23°10	19°35	27°50	22°40	28°40	0°41	28°17	1°55	3°37	23°R57	23°21	7°40	25°50	W 4
T 5	16 54 42	14°36'12	5♎10	21°44	28°49	23°12	28°54	0°44	28°20	1°56	3°36	23°56	23°17	7°47	25°53	T 5
F 6	16 58 39	15°33'38	17° 1	23°52	29°48	23°45	29° 7	0°48	28°24	1°57	3°35	23°54	23°14	7°54	25°55	F 6
S 7	17 2 35	16°31'03	28°50	25°58	0♉48	24°17	29°21	0°52	28°27	1°58	3°34	23°50	23°11	8° 1	25°58	S 7
S 8	17 6 32	17°28'27	10♏39	28° 3	1°48	24°50	29°35	0°55	28°30	1°59	3°33	23°44	23° 8	8° 7	26° 0	S 8
M 9	17 10 28	18°25'50	22°33	0♋ 5	2°48	25°23	29°48	0°58	28°34	2° 0	3°33	23°34	23° 5	8°14	26° 3	M 9
T 10	17 14 25	19°23'11	4♐33	2° 6	3°49	25°55	0♋ 2	1° 2	28°37	2° 0	3°32	23°22	23° 2	8°21	26° 5	T 10
W11	17 18 21	20°20'33	16°42	4° 4	4°50	26°28	0°15	1° 5	28°40	2° 1	3°31	23° 9	22°58	8°27	26° 8	W11
T 12	17 22 18	21°17'53	29° 1	6° 1	5°51	27° 1	0°29	1° 8	28°44	2° 2	3°30	22°56	22°55	8°34	26°10	T 12
F 13	17 26 15	22°15'12	11♑29	7°55	6°52	27°35	0°43	1°11	28°47	2° 3	3°29	22°43	22°52	8°41	26°12	F 13
S 14	17 30 11	23°12'31	24° 8	9°46	7°54	28° 8	0°56	1°14	28°50	2° 3	3°28	22°33	22°49	8°47	26°15	S 14
S 15	17 34 8	24° 9'50	6♒58	11°36	8°56	28°41	1°10	1°17	28°53	2° 4	3°27	22°24	22°46	8°54	26°17	S 15
M16	17 38 4	25° 7'08	20° 0	13°22	9°58	29°14	1°24	1°19	28°57	2° 5	3°26	22°19	22°42	9° 1	26°19	M16
T 17	17 42 1	26° 4'25	3♓15	15° 7	11° 1	29°48	1°37	1°22	29° 0	2° 5	3°25	22°16	22°39	9° 7	26°21	T 17
W18	17 45 57	27° 1'43	16°45	16°49	12° 4	0♍22	1°51	1°24	29° 3	2° 6	3°24	22°16	22°36	9°14	26°23	W18
T 19	17 49 54	27°58'59	0♈30	18°29	13° 7	0°55	2° 5	1°27	29° 6	2° 6	3°23	22°16	22°33	9°21	26°25	T 19
F 20	17 53 50	28°56'16	14°33	20° 6	14°10	1°29	2°18	1°29	29° 9	2° 7	3°22	22°15	22°30	9°27	26°27	F 20
S 21	17 57 47	29°53'33	28°52	21°41	15°14	2° 3	2°32	1°31	29°12	2° 7	3°20	22°13	22°27	9°34	26°29	S 21
S 22	18 1 44	0♋50'49	13♉26	23°13	16°17	2°37	2°46	1°34	29°16	2° 8	3°19	22° 8	22°23	9°41	26°31	S 22
M23	18 5 40	1°48'06	28°11	24°43	17°21	3°11	2°59	1°36	29°19	2° 8	3°18	22° 1	22°20	9°48	26°33	M23
T 24	18 9 37	2°45'22	12♊59	26°10	18°26	3°45	3°13	1°38	29°22	2° 9	3°17	21°52	22°17	9°54	26°35	T 24
W25	18 13 33	3°42'38	27°43	27°34	19°30	4°19	3°27	1°39	29°25	2° 9	3°16	21°41	22°14	10° 1	26°37	W25
T 26	18 17 30	4°39'54	12♋15	28°56	20°35	4°53	3°41	1°41	29°28	2° 9	3°15	21°30	22°11	10° 8	26°39	T 26
F 27	18 21 26	5°37'09	26°27	0♌16	21°39	5°28	3°54	1°43	29°31	2°10	3°13	21°20	22° 8	10°14	26°40	F 27
S 28	18 25 23	6°34'24	10♌16	1°33	22°44	6° 2	4° 8	1°44	29°34	2°10	3°12	21°12	22° 4	10°21	26°42	S 28
S 29	18 29 19	7°31'38	23°38	2°47	23°49	6°37	4°22	1°46	29°37	2°10	3°11	21° 7	22° 1	10°28	26°44	S 29
M30	18 33 16	8♋28'52	6♍34	3♌58	24♉55	7♍11	4♋35	1♈47	29♉40	2♈10	3♒10	21♓ 5	21♓58	10♏34	26♈45	M30

JULY 2025 00:00 UT

Day	Sid.t	☉	☽	☿	♀	♂	♃	♄	♅	♆	♇	☊	☊	⚸	⚷	Day
T 1	18 37 13	9♋26'06	19♍ 8	5♌ 6	26♉ 0	7♍46	4♋49	1♈49	29♉42	2♈10	3°R 8	21°D 4	21♓55	10♏41	26♈47	T 1
W 2	18 41 9	10°23'19	1♎23	6°12	27° 6	8°21	5° 3	1°50	29°45	2°10	3♒ 7	21♓ 4	21°52	10°48	26°48	W 2
T 3	18 45 6	11°20'32	13°24	7°14	28°11	8°56	5°16	1°51	29°48	2°10	3° 6	21°R 4	21°48	10°54	26°50	T 3
F 4	18 49 2	12°17'44	25°17	8°14	29°17	9°31	5°30	1°52	29°51	2°11	3° 5	21° 3	21°45	11° 1	26°51	F 4
S 5	18 52 59	13°14'56	7♏ 7	9°10	0♊23	10° 6	5°44	1°53	29°54	2°R11	3° 3	21° 1	21°42	11° 8	26°53	S 5
S 6	18 56 55	14°12'08	18°59	10° 3	1°30	10°41	5°57	1°53	29°56	2°11	3° 2	20°56	21°39	11°14	26°54	S 6
M 7	19 0 52	15° 9'20	0♐57	10°52	2°36	11°16	6°11	1°54	29°59	2°10	3° 1	20°48	21°36	11°21	26°55	M 7
T 8	19 4 48	16° 6'32	13° 4	11°38	3°43	11°51	6°24	1°55	0♊ 2	2°10	2°59	20°39	21°33	11°28	26°56	T 8
W 9	19 8 45	17° 3'44	25°22	12°21	4°49	12°26	6°38	1°55	0° 4	2°10	2°58	20°28	21°29	11°35	26°57	W 9
T 10	19 12 42	18° 0'55	7♑54	12°59	5°56	13° 2	6°51	1°56	0° 7	2°10	2°57	20°17	21°26	11°41	26°59	T 10
F 11	19 16 38	18°58'07	20°39	13°34	7° 3	13°37	7° 5	1°56	0°10	2°10	2°55	20° 7	21°23	11°48	27° 0	F 11
S 12	19 20 35	19°55'19	3♒37	14° 4	8°10	14°13	7°19	1°56	0°12	2°10	2°54	19°58	21°20	11°55	27° 1	S 12
S 13	19 24 31	20°52'32	16°47	14°31	9°17	14°48	7°32	1°R56	0°15	2° 9	2°53	19°51	21°17	12° 1	27° 2	S 13
M14	19 28 28	21°49'44	0♓ 8	14°52	10°25	15°24	7°45	1°56	0°17	2° 9	2°51	19°47	21°14	12° 8	27° 2	M14
T 15	19 32 24	22°46'57	13°41	15°10	11°32	16° 0	7°59	1°56	0°20	2° 9	2°50	19°D46	21°10	12°15	27° 3	T 15
W16	19 36 21	23°44'11	27°23	15°23	12°40	16°36	8°12	1°56	0°22	2° 9	2°48	19°46	21° 7	12°21	27° 4	W16
T 17	19 40 18	24°41'25	11♈16	15°31	13°48	17°11	8°26	1°55	0°24	2° 8	2°47	19°47	21° 4	12°28	27° 5	T 17
F 18	19 44 14	25°38'40	25°18	15°R34	14°56	17°47	8°39	1°55	0°27	2° 8	2°46	19°R47	21° 1	12°35	27° 6	F 18
S 19	19 48 11	26°35'55	9♉29	15°33	16° 4	18°23	8°52	1°54	0°29	2° 7	2°44	19°46	20°58	12°42	27° 6	S 19
S 20	19 52 7	27°33'12	23°48	15°27	17°12	18°59	9° 6	1°54	0°31	2° 7	2°43	19°44	20°54	12°48	27° 7	S 20
M21	19 56 4	28°30'29	8♊11	15°15	18°20	19°36	9°19	1°53	0°33	2° 6	2°41	19°39	20°51	12°55	27° 7	M21
T 22	20 0 0	29°27'47	22°34	14°59	19°28	20°12	9°32	1°52	0°36	2° 6	2°40	19°33	20°48	13° 2	27° 8	T 22
W23	20 3 57	0♌25'06	6♋53	14°39	20°37	20°48	9°46	1°51	0°38	2° 5	2°39	19°25	20°45	13° 8	27° 8	W23
T 24	20 7 53	1°22'25	21° 1	14°14	21°46	21°25	9°59	1°50	0°40	2° 5	2°37	19°17	20°42	13°15	27° 9	T 24
F 25	20 11 50	2°19'45	4♌54	13°44	22°54	22° 1	10°12	1°49	0°42	2° 4	2°36	19°11	20°39	13°22	27° 9	F 25
S 26	20 15 47	3°17'06	18°28	13°11	24° 3	22°38	10°25	1°48	0°44	2° 3	2°34	19° 5	20°35	13°28	27° 9	S 26
S 27	20 19 43	4°14'27	1♍40	12°34	25°12	23°14	10°38	1°46	0°46	2° 3	2°33	19° 2	20°32	13°35	27° 9	S 27
M28	20 23 40	5°11'49	14°32	11°55	26°21	23°51	10°51	1°45	0°48	2° 2	2°32	19°D 0	20°29	13°42	27°10	M28
T 29	20 27 36	6° 9'11	27° 4	11°13	27°30	24°27	11° 4	1°43	0°50	2° 1	2°30	19° 1	20°26	13°48	27°10	T 29
W30	20 31 33	7° 6'34	9♎19	10°29	28°39	25° 4	11°17	1°42	0°52	2° 1	2°29	19° 2	20°23	13°55	27°10	W30
T 31	20 35 29	8♌ 3'57	21♎21	9♌45	29♊49	25♍41	11♋30	1♈40	0♊54	2♈ 0	2♒27	19♓ 3	20♓20	14♏ 2	27°R10	T 31

AUGUST 2025

00:00 UT

Day	Sid.t	☉	☽	☿	♀	♂	♃	♄	♅	♆	♇	☊	☊	⚸	⚷	Day
F 1	20 39 26	9♌ 1'21	3♏15	9°R 0	0♋58	26♍18	11♋43	1°R38	0♊55	1°R59	2°R26	19♓ 4	20♓16	14♏ 9	27°R10	F 1
S 2	20 43 22	9°58'45	15° 7	8♌16	2° 7	26°55	11°56	1♈36	0°57	1♈58	2♒24	19°R 4	20°13	14°15	27♈10	S 2
S 3	20 47 19	10°56'10	27° 0	7°34	3°17	27°32	12° 8	1°34	0°59	1°57	2°23	19° 3	20°10	14°22	27° 9	S 3
M 4	20 51 16	11°53'36	9♐ 1	6°53	4°27	28° 9	12°21	1°32	1° 0	1°56	2°22	19° 0	20° 7	14°29	27° 9	M 4
T 5	20 55 12	12°51'03	21°12	6°16	5°37	28°46	12°34	1°30	1° 2	1°55	2°20	18°56	20° 4	14°35	27° 9	T 5
W 6	20 59 9	13°48'30	3♑37	5°43	6°46	29°24	12°46	1°28	1° 3	1°54	2°19	18°50	20° 0	14°42	27° 9	W 6
T 7	21 3 5	14°45'58	16°18	5°14	7°56	0♎ 1	12°59	1°26	1° 5	1°53	2°18	18°44	19°57	14°49	27° 8	T 7
F 8	21 7 2	15°43'27	29°17	4°51	9° 6	0°38	13°11	1°23	1° 6	1°52	2°16	18°39	19°54	14°55	27° 8	F 8
S 9	21 10 58	16°40'57	12♒34	4°33	10°17	1°16	13°24	1°21	1° 8	1°51	2°15	18°35	19°51	15° 2	27° 7	S 9
S 10	21 14 55	17°38'28	26° 6	4°21	11°27	1°53	13°36	1°18	1° 9	1°50	2°13	18°31	19°48	15° 9	27° 7	S 10
M11	21 18 51	18°36'00	9♓52	4°D15	12°37	2°31	13°49	1°15	1°11	1°49	2°12	18°30	19°45	15°16	27° 6	M11
T 12	21 22 48	19°33'33	23°49	4°17	13°48	3° 8	14° 1	1°12	1°12	1°48	2°11	18°D30	19°41	15°22	27° 6	T 12
W13	21 26 45	20°31'07	7♈55	4°25	14°58	3°46	14°13	1°10	1°13	1°47	2° 9	18°31	19°38	15°29	27° 5	W13
T 14	21 30 41	21°28'43	22° 5	4°40	16° 9	4°24	14°25	1° 7	1°14	1°46	2° 8	18°32	19°35	15°36	27° 4	T 14
F 15	21 34 38	22°26'20	6♉18	5° 3	17°19	5° 2	14°37	1° 4	1°15	1°45	2° 7	18°33	19°32	15°42	27° 4	F 15
S 16	21 38 34	23°23'59	20°32	5°32	18°30	5°40	14°49	1° 0	1°16	1°44	2° 6	18°R34	19°29	15°49	27° 3	S 16
S 17	21 42 31	24°21'40	4♊43	6° 9	19°41	6°18	15° 1	0°57	1°18	1°42	2° 4	18°34	19°25	15°56	27° 2	S 17
M18	21 46 27	25°19'22	18°51	6°53	20°52	6°56	15°13	0°54	1°18	1°41	2° 3	18°32	19°22	16° 2	27° 1	M18
T 19	21 50 24	26°17'06	2♋52	7°44	22° 3	7°34	15°25	0°51	1°19	1°40	2° 2	18°30	19°19	16° 9	27° 0	T 19
W20	21 54 20	27°14'52	16°44	8°42	23°14	8°12	15°37	0°47	1°20	1°39	2° 0	18°27	19°16	16°16	26°59	W20
T 21	21 58 17	28°12'39	0♌25	9°46	24°25	8°50	15°49	0°44	1°21	1°37	1°59	18°24	19°13	16°23	26°58	T 21
F 22	22 2 14	29°10'27	13°52	10°56	25°37	9°28	16° 0	0°40	1°22	1°36	1°58	18°22	19°10	16°29	26°57	F 22
S 23	22 6 10	0♍ 8'17	27° 4	12°13	26°48	10° 7	16°12	0°37	1°23	1°35	1°57	18°20	19° 6	16°36	26°56	S 23
S 24	22 10 7	1° 6'08	10♍ 0	13°35	27°59	10°45	16°23	0°33	1°23	1°33	1°56	18°19	19° 3	16°43	26°54	S 24
M25	22 14 3	2° 4'01	22°40	15° 2	29°11	11°24	16°35	0°29	1°24	1°32	1°54	18°D19	19° 0	16°49	26°53	M25
T 26	22 18 0	3° 1'55	5♎ 4	16°34	0♌23	12° 2	16°46	0°25	1°25	1°30	1°53	18°19	18°57	16°56	26°52	T 26
W27	22 21 56	3°59'50	17°16	18°11	1°34	12°41	16°57	0°22	1°25	1°29	1°52	18°20	18°54	17° 3	26°50	W27
T 28	22 25 53	4°57'47	29°17	19°51	2°46	13°19	17° 9	0°18	1°26	1°28	1°51	18°22	18°51	17° 9	26°49	T 28
F 29	22 29 49	5°55'45	11♏11	21°35	3°58	13°58	17°20	0°14	1°26	1°26	1°50	18°23	18°47	17°16	26°47	F 29
S 30	22 33 46	6°53'44	23° 2	23°22	5°10	14°37	17°31	0°10	1°26	1°25	1°49	18°24	18°44	17°23	26°46	S 30
S 31	22 37 43	7♍51'45	4♐56	25♌11	6♌22	15♎16	17♋42	0♈ 6	1♊27	1♈23	1♒48	18°R24	18♓41	17♏30	26♈44	S 31

SEPTEMBER 2025   00:00 UT

Day	Sid.t	☉	☽	☿	♀	♂	♃	♄	⛢	♆	♇	☊	♆	⚷	δ
M 1	22 41 39	8♏49'47	16♓55	27♌ 3	7♎34	15♌24	17♋52	0♓R 1	1Ⅱ27	1♈R22	19°47	18°R24	18♓38	17♏36	26°R43
T 2	22 45 36	9 47'51	29° 6	28°56	8 46	16 34	18° 3	29♓57	1 27	1 20	1♑45	18 23	18 35	17 43	26°41
W 3	22 49 32	10 45'56	11♏33	0♏51	9 58	17 13	18 14	29 53	1 28	1 19	1 44	18 23	18 31	17 50	26 39
T 4	22 53 29	11 44'02	24 18	2 46	11 10	17 52	18 24	29 49	1 28	1 18	1 43	18 22	18 28	17 56	26 38
F 5	22 57 25	12 42'10	7♐24	4 42	12 22	18 31	18 35	29 45	1 28	1 17	1 42	18 21	18 25	18 3	26 36
S 6	23 1 22	13 40'19	20 52	6 39	13 35	19 10	18 45	29 40	1°R28	1 16	1 41	18 20	18 22	18 10	26 34
S 7	23 5 18	14 38'30	4♑42	8 35	14 47	19 50	18 55	29 36	1 28	1 14	1 40	18°D20	18 19	18 16	26 32
M 8	23 9 15	15 36'43	18 51	10 31	16 0	20 29	19° 5	29 31	1 28	1 12	1 40	18°D20	18 16	18 23	26 30
T 9	23 13 12	16 34'57	3♒15	12 27	17 12	21 8	19 16	29 27	1 28	1 11	1 39	18 20	18 12	18 30	26 28
W10	23 17 8	17 33'13	17 48	14 22	18 25	21 48	19 25	29 22	1 27	1 10	1 38	18 20	18° 9	18 37	26 26
T11	23 21 5	18 31'31	2♓28	16 17	19 37	22 27	19 35	29 18	1 27	1 9	1 37	18°R20	18° 6	18 43	26 24
F12	23 25 1	19 29'51	16 58	18 11	20 50	23 7	19 45	29 13	1 27	1 8	1 36	18 20	18° 3	18 50	26 22
S13	23 28 58	20 28'14	1Ⅱ25	20° 4	22° 3	23 47	19 55	29° 9	1 27	1 6	1 35	18 20	18° 0	18 57	26 20
S14	23 32 54	21 26'38	15 40	21°56	23°16	24 26	20° 4	29° 4	1 26	1 5	1 34	18°D20	17 57	19° 3	26 18
M15	23 36 51	22 25'05	29 42	23 47	25° 6	25° 6	20 13	28 59	1 26	1 4	1 34	18 20	17 53	19 10	26 16
T16	23 40 47	23 23'34	13♋30	25 37	25 42	25 46	20 23	28 55	1 25	1 3	1 33	18 21	17 50	19 17	26 14
W17	23 44 44	24 22'05	27° 2	27 27	26 55	26 26	20 32	28 50	1 25	1 1	1 32	18 21	17 47	19 24	26 12
T18	23 48 41	25 20'38	10♌19	29°15	28° 8	27° 6	20 41	28 46	1 24	1 0	1 31	18 21	17 44	19 30	26°10
F19	23 52 37	26 19'13	23 21	1♎ 2	29 21	27 46	20 50	28 41	1 23	0 58	1 30	18 22	17 41	19 37	26° 7
S20	23 56 34	27 17'50	6♏11	2 48	0♏35	28 26	20 59	28 36	1 23	0 57	1 30	18 22	17 37	19 44	26° 5
S21	0 0 30	28 16'29	18 47	4 33	1 48	29° 6	21° 8	28 32	1 22	0 55	1 29	18°R23	17 34	19 50	26° 2
M22	0 4 27	29 15'11	1♎11	6 17	3° 1	29 47	21 16	28 27	1 22	0 54	1 29	18 22	17 31	19 57	26° 0
T23	0 8 23	0♎13'54	13 25	8° 0	4°15	0♏27	21 25	28 22	1 21	0 53	1 28	18 21	17 28	20° 4	25°58
W24	0 12 20	1 12'39	25°30	9 43	5 28	1° 7	21 33	28 18	1 20	0 51	1 27	18 20	17 25	20°10	25 55
T25	0 16 16	2 11'26	7♏27	11 24	6 42	1 48	21 41	28 13	1 19	0 48	1 27	18 20	17 22	20°17	25 53
F26	0 20 13	3 10'14	19 20	13° 4	7 55	2 28	21 49	28° 8	1 18	0 45	1 27	18 18	17 18	20 24	25 50
S27	0 24 9	4° 9'05	1♐11	14°43	9° 9	3° 9	21 57	28° 4	1 17	0 41	1 27	18 16	17 15	20 31	25°48
S28	0 28 6	5° 7'57	13° 3	16 22	10 23	3 50	22° 5	27 59	1 16	0 38	1 26	18 13	17 12	20°37	25°45
M29	0 32 3	6° 6'51	25° 1	17°59	11 37	4 30	22 13	27 55	1 15	0 36	1 25	18 12	17° 9	20 44	25°43
T30	0 35 59	7♎ 5'47	7♑ 9	19♎36	12♏50	5♏11	22♋20	27♓50	1Ⅱ14	0♈35	1♑25	18°D10	17♓ 6	20♏51	25°40

Day
M 1
T 2
W 3
T 4
F 5
S 6
S 7
M 8
T 9
W10
T11
F12
S13
S14
M15
T16
W17
T18
F19
S20
S21
M22
T23
W24
T25
F26
S27
S28
M29
T30

78

OCTOBER 2025 00:00 UT

Day	Sid.t	☉	☽	☿	♀	♂	♃	♄	♅	♆	♇	☊	☊	⚸	⚷	Day
W 1	0 39 56	8♎ 4'45	19♑31	21♎11	14♍ 4	5♏52	22♋28	27°R45	1°R13	0°R33	1°R24	18♓10	17♓ 3	20♏57	25°R37	W 1
T 2	0 43 52	9° 3'45	2♒13	22°46	15°18	6°33	22°35	27♓41	1♊11	0♈31	1♒24	18°12	16°59	21° 4	25♈35	T 2
F 3	0 47 49	10° 2'46	15°17	24°20	16°32	7°14	22°42	27°36	1°10	0°30	1°24	18°13	16°56	21°11	25°32	F 3
S 4	0 51 45	11° 1'48	28°47	25°53	17°46	7°55	22°49	27°32	1° 9	0°28	1°23	18°14	16°53	21°18	25°30	S 4
S 5	0 55 42	12° 0'53	12♓44	27°25	19° 0	8°36	22°56	27°28	1° 7	0°27	1°23	18°R15	16°50	21°24	25°27	S 5
M 6	0 59 38	13° 0'00	27° 5	28°57	20°14	9°17	23° 3	27°23	1° 6	0°25	1°23	18°15	16°47	21°31	25°24	M 6
T 7	1 3 35	13°59'08	11♈47	0♏28	21°28	9°58	23° 9	27°19	1° 5	0°23	1°23	18°14	16°43	21°38	25°22	T 7
W 8	1 7 32	14°58'18	26°44	1°57	22°42	10°39	23°15	27°14	1° 3	0°22	1°23	18°11	16°40	21°44	25°19	W 8
T 9	1 11 28	15°57'31	11♉47	3°26	23°57	11°21	23°22	27°10	1° 2	0°20	1°22	18° 7	16°37	21°51	25°16	T 9
F 10	1 15 25	16°56'46	26°46	4°55	25°11	12° 2	23°28	27° 6	1° 0	0°19	1°22	18° 3	16°34	21°58	25°13	F 10
S 11	1 19 21	17°56'03	11♊34	6°22	26°25	12°43	23°34	27° 2	0°58	0°17	1°22	18° 0	16°31	22° 4	25°11	S 11
S 12	1 23 18	18°55'23	26° 4	7°49	27°40	13°25	23°39	26°58	0°57	0°15	1°22	17°57	16°28	22°11	25° 8	S 12
M13	1 27 14	19°54'44	10♋12	9°15	28°54	14° 6	23°45	26°53	0°55	0°14	1°22	17°55	16°24	22°18	25° 5	M13
T 14	1 31 11	20°54'09	23°57	10°39	0♎ 8	14°48	23°50	26°49	0°53	0°12	1°D22	17°D54	16°21	22°25	25° 2	T 14
W15	1 35 7	21°53'35	7♌19	12° 3	1°23	15°30	23°56	26°45	0°52	0°11	1°22	17°55	16°18	22°31	25° 0	W15
T 16	1 39 4	22°53'04	20°22	13°27	2°37	16°12	24° 1	26°41	0°50	0° 9	1°22	17°57	16°15	22°38	24°57	T 16
F 17	1 43 1	23°52'35	3♍ 7	14°49	3°52	16°53	24° 6	26°38	0°48	0° 8	1°22	17°58	16°12	22°45	24°54	F 17
S 18	1 46 57	24°52'08	15°38	16°10	5° 6	17°35	24°10	26°34	0°46	0° 6	1°22	17°R59	16° 8	22°51	24°51	S 18
S 19	1 50 54	25°51'43	27°57	17°30	6°21	18°17	24°15	26°30	0°44	0° 5	1°22	17°59	16° 5	22°58	24°48	S 19
M20	1 54 50	26°51'20	10♎ 7	18°49	7°36	18°59	24°19	26°26	0°42	0° 3	1°23	17°56	16° 2	23° 5	24°46	M20
T 21	1 58 47	27°51'00	22°10	20° 7	8°50	19°41	24°24	26°23	0°40	0° 2	1°23	17°52	15°59	23°12	24°43	T 21
W22	2 2 43	28°50'42	4♏ 7	21°23	10° 5	20°23	24°28	26°19	0°38	0° 1	1°23	17°46	15°56	23°18	24°40	W22
T 23	2 6 40	29°50'25	16° 1	22°38	11°20	21° 6	24°31	26°16	0°36	29♓59	1°23	17°38	15°53	23°25	24°37	T 23
F 24	2 10 36	0♏50'11	27°52	23°52	12°35	21°48	24°35	26°12	0°34	29°58	1°23	17°30	15°49	23°32	24°35	F 24
S 25	2 14 33	1°49'58	9♐43	25° 4	13°49	22°30	24°39	26° 9	0°32	29°56	1°24	17°21	15°46	23°38	24°32	S 25
S 26	2 18 30	2°49'47	21°36	26°14	15° 4	23°13	24°42	26° 6	0°30	29°55	1°24	17°13	15°43	23°45	24°29	S 26
M27	2 22 26	3°49'38	3♑33	27°22	16°19	23°55	24°45	26° 2	0°28	29°54	1°24	17° 7	15°40	23°52	24°26	M27
T 28	2 26 23	4°49'31	15°39	28°28	17°34	24°38	24°48	25°59	0°26	29°52	1°25	17° 3	15°37	23°59	24°24	T 28
W29	2 30 19	5°49'26	27°58	29°32	18°49	25°20	24°51	25°56	0°23	29°51	1°25	17° 1	15°34	24° 5	24°21	W29
T 30	2 34 16	6°49'22	10♒33	0♐33	20° 4	26° 3	24°53	25°53	0°21	29°50	1°26	17°D 1	15°30	24°12	24°18	T 30
F 31	2 38 12	7♏49'19	23♒30	1♐31	21♎19	26♏45	24♋56	25♓51	0♊19	29♓49	1♒26	17♓ 1	15♓27	24♏19	24♈16	F 31

NOVEMBER 2025

00:00 UT

Day	Sid.t	☉	☽	☿	♀	♂	♃	♄	♅	♆	♇	☊	☊	⚸	⚷	Day
S 1	2 42 9	8♏49'18	6♓52	2♐25	22♎34	27♏28	24♋58	25°R48	0°R17	29°R48	1♒27	17♓ 3	15♓24	24♏25	24°R13	S 1
S 2	2 46 5	9°49'19	20°43	3°16	23°49	28°11	25° 0	25♓45	0♊14	29♓46	1°27	17°R 3	15°21	24°32	24♈10	S 2
M 3	2 50 2	10°49'21	5♈ 2	4° 3	25° 4	28°54	25° 2	25°42	0°12	29°45	1°28	17° 1	15°18	24°39	24° 8	M 3
T 4	2 53 59	11°49'25	19°48	4°46	26°19	29°37	25° 3	25°40	0°10	29°44	1°28	16°58	15°14	24°46	24° 5	T 4
W 5	2 57 55	12°49'31	4♉54	5°23	27°34	0♐20	25° 5	25°38	0° 7	29°43	1°29	16°52	15°11	24°52	24° 2	W 5
T 6	3 1 52	13°49'39	20°12	5°54	28°49	1° 3	25° 6	25°35	0° 5	29°42	1°30	16°44	15° 8	24°59	24° 0	T 6
F 7	3 5 48	14°49'48	5♊31	6°20	0♏ 4	1°46	25° 7	25°33	0° 3	29°41	1°30	16°35	15° 5	25° 6	23°57	F 7
S 8	3 9 45	15°50'00	20°39	6°38	1°19	2°29	25° 8	25°31	0° 0	29°40	1°31	16°26	15° 2	25°12	23°55	S 8
S 9	3 13 41	16°50'13	5♋26	6°49	2°34	3°12	25° 8	25°29	29♉58	29°39	1°32	16°18	14°59	25°19	23°52	S 9
M10	3 17 38	17°50'28	19°48	6°R52	3°50	3°55	25° 9	25°27	29°55	29°38	1°32	16°13	14°55	25°26	23°50	M10
T 11	3 21 34	18°50'46	3♌41	6°45	5° 5	4°39	25° 9	25°25	29°53	29°37	1°33	16° 9	14°52	25°33	23°47	T 11
W12	3 25 31	19°51'05	17° 5	6°29	6°20	5°22	25°R 9	25°23	29°50	29°36	1°34	16°D 8	14°49	25°39	23°45	W12
T 13	3 29 28	20°51'26	0♍ 4	6° 3	7°35	6° 6	25° 9	25°22	29°48	29°35	1°35	16° 8	14°46	25°46	23°43	T 13
F 14	3 33 24	21°51'49	12°42	5°27	8°51	6°49	25° 9	25°20	29°46	29°34	1°36	16°R 9	14°43	25°53	23°40	F 14
S 15	3 37 21	22°52'14	25° 3	4°41	10° 6	7°33	25° 8	25°19	29°43	29°33	1°37	16° 9	14°40	25°59	23°38	S 15
S 16	3 41 17	23°52'41	7♎12	3°45	11°21	8°16	25° 7	25°17	29°41	29°32	1°37	16° 6	14°36	26° 6	23°35	S 16
M17	3 45 14	24°53'10	19°12	2°41	12°36	9° 0	25° 6	25°16	29°38	29°32	1°38	16° 2	14°33	26°13	23°33	M17
T 18	3 49 10	25°53'40	1♏ 7	1°29	13°52	9°44	25° 5	25°15	29°36	29°31	1°39	15°54	14°30	26°20	23°31	T 18
W19	3 53 7	26°54'13	12°59	0°11	15° 7	10°28	25° 4	25°14	29°33	29°30	1°40	15°43	14°27	26°26	23°29	W19
T 20	3 57 3	27°54'46	24°51	28♏50	16°22	11°11	25° 2	25°13	29°31	29°29	1°41	15°30	14°24	26°33	23°27	T 20
F 21	4 1 0	28°55'22	6♐43	27°29	17°38	11°55	25° 0	25°12	29°28	29°29	1°42	15°16	14°20	26°40	23°24	F 21
S 22	4 4 57	29°55'59	18°36	26°10	18°53	12°39	24°58	25°11	29°26	29°28	1°43	15° 2	14°17	26°46	23°22	S 22
S 23	4 8 53	0♐56'37	0♑34	24°55	20° 9	13°23	24°56	25°11	29°23	29°28	1°45	14°49	14°14	26°53	23°20	S 23
M24	4 12 50	1°57'16	12°36	23°48	21°24	14° 7	24°54	25°10	29°21	29°27	1°46	14°38	14°11	27° 0	23°18	M24
T 25	4 16 46	2°57'57	24°45	22°49	22°39	14°52	24°51	25°10	29°18	29°26	1°47	14°29	14° 8	27° 7	23°16	T 25
W26	4 20 43	3°58'39	7♒ 5	22° 1	23°55	15°36	24°49	25°10	29°15	29°26	1°48	14°24	14° 5	27°13	23°14	W26
T 27	4 24 39	4°59'22	19°38	21°24	25°10	16°20	24°46	25°10	29°13	29°25	1°49	14°21	14° 1	27°20	23°12	T 27
F 28	4 28 36	6° 0'06	2♓30	20°59	26°26	17° 4	24°43	25°D 9	29°11	29°25	1°50	14°D20	13°58	27°27	23°10	F 28
S 29	4 32 32	7° 0'51	15°43	20°45	27°41	17°49	24°39	25° 9	29° 8	29°25	1°52	14°R20	13°55	27°34	23° 9	S 29
S 30	4 36 29	8♐ 1'36	29♓21	20°D43	28♏56	18♐33	24♋36	25♓10	29♉ 6	29♓24	1♒53	14♓20	13♓52	27♏40	23♈ 7	S 30

DECEMBER 2025 — 00:00 UT

Day	Sid.t	☉	☽	☿	♀	♂	♃	♄	♅	♆	♇	☊	Ω	⚸	⚷	Day
M 1	4 40 26	9♐ 2'23	13♈27	20♏51	0♐12	19♐18	24°R32	25♓10	29°R 3	29°R24	1♒54	14°R17	13♓49	27♏47	23°R 5	M 1
T 2	4 44 22	10° 3'11	28° 1	21° 8	1°27	20° 2	24♋28	25°10	29♉ 1	29♓24	1°55	14♓13	13°46	27°54	23♈ 3	T 2
W 3	4 48 19	11° 3'59	12♉59	21°35	2°43	20°47	24°24	25°11	28°58	29°23	1°57	14° 5	13°42	28° 0	23° 2	W 3
T 4	4 52 15	12° 4'49	28°13	22°10	3°58	21°31	24°20	25°11	28°56	29°23	1°58	13°55	13°39	28° 7	23° 0	T 4
F 5	4 56 12	13° 5'40	13♊33	22°52	5°14	22°16	24°15	25°12	28°53	29°23	1°59	13°43	13°36	28°14	22°59	F 5
S 6	5 0 8	14° 6'32	28°48	23°40	6°29	23° 1	24°11	25°13	28°51	29°23	2° 1	13°31	13°33	28°21	22°57	S 6
S 7	5 4 5	15° 7'25	13♋46	24°33	7°45	23°46	24° 6	25°14	28°49	29°23	2° 2	13°21	13°30	28°27	22°56	S 7
M 8	5 8 2	16° 8'19	28°20	25°32	9° 0	24°30	24° 1	25°15	28°46	29°22	2° 4	13°13	13°26	28°34	22°54	M 8
T 9	5 11 58	17° 9'15	12♌24	26°35	10°16	25°15	23°56	25°16	28°44	29°22	2° 5	13° 8	13°23	28°41	22°53	T 9
W10	5 15 55	18°10'11	25°57	27°42	11°31	26° 0	23°51	25°17	28°41	29°22	2° 7	13° 5	13°20	28°47	22°52	W10
T 11	5 19 51	19°11'09	9♍ 2	28°51	12°47	26°45	23°45	25°18	28°39	29°D22	2° 8	13° 4	13°17	28°54	22°50	T 11
F 12	5 23 48	20°12'07	21°42	0♐ 4	14° 2	27°30	23°40	25°20	28°37	29°22	2°10	13° 4	13°14	29° 1	22°49	F 12
S 13	5 27 44	21°13'07	4♎ 3	1°19	15°18	28°15	23°34	25°21	28°35	29°22	2°11	13° 4	13°11	29° 8	22°48	S 13
S 14	5 31 41	22°14'08	16° 9	2°36	16°33	29° 1	23°28	25°23	28°32	29°23	2°13	13° 2	13° 7	29°14	22°47	S 14
M15	5 35 37	23°15'10	28° 6	3°56	17°49	29°46	23°22	25°25	28°30	29°23	2°14	12°57	13° 4	29°21	22°46	M15
T 16	5 39 34	24°16'13	9♏57	5°16	19° 4	0♑31	23°16	25°27	28°28	29°23	2°16	12°49	13° 1	29°28	22°45	T 16
W17	5 43 31	25°17'17	21°47	6°38	20°20	1°16	23°10	25°29	28°26	29°23	2°17	12°39	12°58	29°34	22°44	W17
T 18	5 47 27	26°18'22	3♐38	8° 1	21°35	2° 2	23° 3	25°31	28°24	29°23	2°19	12°26	12°55	29°41	22°43	T 18
F 19	5 51 24	27°19'27	15°33	9°26	22°51	2°47	22°57	25°33	28°21	29°24	2°21	12°12	12°52	29°48	22°42	F 19
S 20	5 55 20	28°20'33	27°33	10°51	24° 6	3°32	22°50	25°35	28°19	29°24	2°22	11°57	12°48	29°55	22°41	S 20
S 21	5 59 17	29°21'40	9♑39	12°17	25°22	4°18	22°43	25°37	28°17	29°24	2°24	11°44	12°45	0♐ 1	22°40	S 21
M22	6 3 13	0♑22'47	21°51	13°44	26°37	5° 4	22°36	25°40	28°15	29°25	2°26	11°32	12°42	0° 8	22°40	M22
T 23	6 7 10	1°23'55	4♒12	15°11	27°53	5°49	22°29	25°42	28°13	29°25	2°27	11°24	12°39	0°15	22°39	T 23
W24	6 11 6	2°25'03	16°42	16°39	29° 8	6°35	22°22	25°45	28°11	29°26	2°29	11°18	12°36	0°22	22°39	W24
T 25	6 15 3	3°26'11	29°23	18° 8	0♑24	7°20	22°15	25°48	28° 9	29°26	2°31	11°16	12°32	0°28	22°38	T 25
F 26	6 19 0	4°27'19	12♓19	19°37	1°39	8° 6	22° 7	25°51	28° 8	29°27	2°32	11°D15	12°29	0°35	22°38	F 26
S 27	6 22 56	5°28'27	25°31	21° 6	2°55	8°52	22° 0	25°54	28° 6	29°27	2°34	11°15	12°26	0°42	22°37	S 27
S 28	6 26 53	6°29'35	9♈ 3	22°36	4°10	9°38	21°52	25°57	28° 4	29°28	2°36	11°R16	12°23	0°48	22°37	S 28
M29	6 30 49	7°30'43	22°56	24° 6	5°26	10°24	21°45	26° 0	28° 2	29°28	2°38	11°14	12°20	0°55	22°37	M29
T 30	6 34 46	8°31'51	7♉12	25°37	6°41	11° 9	21°37	26° 3	28° 0	29°29	2°40	11°11	12°17	1° 2	22°36	T 30
W31	6 38 42	9♑32'59	21♉50	27♐ 8	7♑57	11♑55	21♋29	26♓ 7	27♉59	29♓30	2♒41	11♓ 5	12♓13	1♐ 9	22♈36	W31

Quick Reference
2025 RETROGRADE MOTION OF PLANETS

MERCURY... Mar 14, 11:45pm 9°♈ .... Apr 7, 4:07am 26°♓
July 17, 9:44pm 15°♌............................ Aug 11th, 12:29am 4°♌
Nov 9, 11:01am 6°♐............................... Nov 29th, 9:38am 20°♏
VENUS......... Mar 1, 4:35pm 10°♈ .... Apr 12, 6:02pm 24°♓
MARS.......... Dec 6, 2024 3:32pm 6°♌ .... Feb 23, 5:59pm 17°♋
JUPITER....... Oct 9, 2024 12:04am 21°♊ .... Feb 4, 1:40am 11°♊
Nov 11, 8:41am 25°♋ .... Mar 10, 2026, 8:29pm 15°♋
SATURN....... Jul 12, 9:07pm 1°♈ .... Nov 27, 7:51pm 25°♓
URANUS...... Sep 1, 2024 8:17am 27°♉ .... Jan 30, 8:22am 23°♉
Sep 5, 9:51pm 1°♊ .... Feb 3, 2026, 6:32pm 27°♉
NEPTUNE.... Jul 4, 2:32pm 2°♈ .... Dec 10, 4:22am 29°♓
PLUTO......... May 4, 8:27am 3°♒ .... Oct 13, 7:52pm 1°♒

2025 ECLIPSES

Mar 13, 11:54pm - Total Lunar 23° ♍ | Mar 29, 3:57am - Partial Solar 9°♈

Sep 7, 11:08am - Total Lunar 15° ♓ | Sep 21, 12:53pm - Partial Solar 29° ♍

Timing: Start projects between the New and Full Moon because energy is rising. The Sun Trine Moon after the Full Moon (Waning Gibbous) is when the energy is flowing most smoothly so that's a good time to overcome resistance. As Planets prepare to change Direction they slow from our perspective and issues related to them in our world will be harder to move forward.

When the Planets are moving fast, you have the wind at your back. Everything related to them happens more quickly and easily. That is why it is important to understand what each Planet signifies. In our Forecasts, we also take into account the speed of the Planets as indicators. Some Planets change Sign and Direction more often.

Quick Reference: Timing

When Planets are above the Dotted Line actions are supported.
Delay these actions when the Planets are below the Dotted Line.

☉ **SUN:** Time to ask favors from superiors, to have dealings with attorneys or government. Start publicity.

☽ **MOON:** Time to handle the public, straighten affairs at home and deal with women. Watch the four quarters of the moon for planting.

☿ **MERCURY:** Start writing, start publishing, start intellectual pursuits, study, learn. Deliver public addresses.

♀ **VENUS:** Commence romance, start to gain favor of the opposite sex. Buy jewelry, clothes. Participate in art, music or entertainment.

♂ **MARS:** Start work on machinery, undergo surgery, start construction, organize sales force. Advance business.

♃ **JUPITER:** Take care of money matters, sign contracts. Start or search for new business. Time to start speculating.

♄ **SATURN:** Start building projects, handle real estate deals, develop mining. Start repairing, plumbing and digging.

♅ **URANUS:** Begin experiments, inventions and new ideas. Start traveling, especially by air. Investigate important propositions.

♆ **NEPTUNE:** Start water trips, start brewing, mix strange chemicals. Start poetry, shipping, investigate secrets.

♇ **PLUTO:** Start organizations, foundations and new principles. Time to "turn over a new leaf."

Quick Reference: Signs & Planetary Rulers

The Twelve Signs

BIRTH DATE SIGN ELEMENT QUALITY RULING PLANET

March 21 to April 19 ..... Aries ♈ ..... Fire ..... Cardinal .... Mars ♂

April 20 to May 20 .... Taurus ♉ ..... Earth .... Fixed ..... Venus ♀

May 21 to June 20 .... Gemini ♊ .... Air .... Mutable .... Mercury ☿

June 21 to July 22 .... Cancer ♋ .... Water .... Cardinal ... Moon ☽

July 23 to August 22 ...... Leo ♌ ..... Fire .... Fixed .... Sun ☉

August 23 to Sept 22 ... Virgo ♍ ... Earth ... Mutable.... Mercury ☿

Sept 23 to Oct 22 ..... Libra ♎ .... Air ..... Cardinal .... Venus ♀

Oct 23 to Nov 21 ...... Scorpio ♏ ..... Water ..... Fixed.....Tr. Mars ♂

                                                  Alternate Ruler - Pluto ♇

Nov 22 to Dec 21 ... Sagittarius ♐ .... Fire .... Mutable .... Jupiter ♃

Dec 22 to Jan 19 .... Capricorn ♑ .... Earth .... Cardinal ... Saturn ♄

Jan 20 to Feb 18 ..... Aquarius ♒ ..... Air ..... Fixed .... Tr. Saturn ♄

                                               Alternate Ruler - Uranus ♅

Feb 19 to March 20 .. Pisces ♓ .... Water.. Mutable... Tr. Jupiter ♃

                                               Alternate Ruler - Neptune ♆

Traditional Ruling Signs from the Table of Dignities (pg. 33) are Signs where the Planet is most socially expressive in a Dynamic or Responsive manner. Note the Exaltation for the Sun is Aries and for the Moon is Taurus. Refer to page 29 for their daily application for Leos and Cancerians.

Calendar Times are based on the Clock for
Pacific Time, changing with Daylight Savings Time.

Books at PlanetaryCalendar.com & Amazon
Planetary Calendar Astrology

Reclaiming Astrology from the Patriarchy
About two millennia ago male priests broke the balanced geometry of Astrology. Then they rebranded the Signs of the Zodiac. These acts elevated men and restricted women's roles in Western society, and we're still using that flawed system today! It's time to restore Astrology's elegant balance and tell the true story of what the stars describe. Look for this book in the Autumn of 2024.

Planetary Calendar Astrology
Moving Beyond Observation Into Action
The calendar's companion book is a complete Astrology course using our practical approach. It uses extensive illustrations and analogies to explain how the chart's geometry and symbolism tell a life story. 172 pages, $20.00 ($3.00 shipping)

The 2025 Lunar Food & Wine Tasting Calendar
The third edition of this calendar is based on BioDynamics. It explains how the Moon Signs affect our enjoyment of food and wine. It offers guidance for timing events and choosing the most suitable meals for every day. The compact design is similar to the Planetary Pocket Calendar. $15.00 ($3.00 shipping)

Feng Shui and the Tango
The Essential Chapters - 25th Anniversary Editon
This includes the easiest to use chapters, that everyone should know from our three book professional series on the environmental healing arts. This will help you create and manage spaces that support your efforts and goals in surprisingly practical ways. 5.5" x 8.5" 107 pages $17.00, ($3.00 shipping) Illustrated ISBN-13: 979-8-838429-85-8

Ordering Next Year's Planetary Calendar

Calendars are ready in the Summer of the current year. Advance orders are mailed as soon as the Calendars are available when pre-paid with a check, money order or credit card. Please include your contact info in case there are questions about your order.
For International orders please email us for a shipping quotes at Sales@SpaceAndTime.com before ordering.

Order Online at www.PlanetaryCalendar.com

**In the USA: XL Wall $20.00   Original Wall $18.00
Mini Pocket $15.00   Day Planner $22.00
Digital for Cell Phones & Tablets $14.00**

U.S. Funds Only - No additional shipping fees required.

MAIL ORDERS TO:
Planetary Calendar
PO Box 5391 Napa, CA 94581-0391
For PHONE ORDERS or CUSTOMER SERVICE Please leave a Voicemail with Email at **(707) 694-8951** - *We respond Quickly!*

We accept AmEx, Disc, MC and Visa via Phone & Online.
Credit card orders require full name, billing address, phone number & email along with credit card #, exp date, & security code.
Please allow 4-6 weeks for delivery (Although they are typically shipped immediately). We are not responsible for postal delays.

Planetary Calendar Since 1949

www.ingramcontent.com/pod-product-compliance
Lightning Source LLC
LaVergne TN
LVHW012033060526
838201LV00061B/4582